I'll Be Happy When ...

How to Lift the Happiness Curse from Your Life

JARED SPRINGER

I'LL BE HAPPY WHEN …

Jared Springer LLC
P.O. Box 928
Washington, UT 84780

www.jaredspringer.com
www.illbehappywhen.com
www.definingmyhappiness.com

Designed by Transcendent Publishing

Edited by Lori Lynn Enterprises

ISBN: 978-1-7359552-0-9

This book is dedicated to my beautiful wife and best friend, Sara. She has always been my biggest cheerleader, encouraging me to shoot for the stars and follow my dreams. I wouldn't be half the man I am today without her never-ending support.

CONTENTS

FOREWORD

Happiness isn't a "where or when," it's a "here and now."

What I thought was just a cute little fortune cookie adage ended up being the catalyst for the greatest spiritual renovation of my life. My name is Nicholas Vescovi, I'm a business owner in California, but I've made a career of delaying my happiness.

I'd spent much of my life saying "I'll be happy when ... " or "when I get _____, then I'll be content," only to be let down as goals came and went ... along with my happiness.

Even the word itself—happiness—is elusive, mysterious, and downright difficult to define. The word "happiness" stems from the word "happenstance," meaning that to be "happy" is contingent on the surroundings or circumstances before you.

This begins a vicious cycle, plaguing many of us, as we find ourselves perplexed like a child in the back seat of the car wondering why no matter how fast we go, we never catch up to the sun.

"What will make me happy?"

"Why am I unhappy?"

Or better yet, "What do I want?"

These were some of the questions I had to ask myself while reading Jared's story ... questions that, quite honestly, I couldn't answer straight away.

Though, as I read his lessons and took the time to peel back the layers, I found that the flight of our joy is not propelled by material gain, nor is it winged by status or position.

The happiness we are after is far more fulfilling and meaningful. It is multicolored and complex while being uniform and simple, like all the pigments that gather to make up a single painting.

Forgiveness, intimacy, relationships, vulnerability, responsibility, fun, gratitude, contentment, community, success, serving, pleasure, peace, purpose, and fulfillment—a full palette of colors that all come together to create the image we call "happy."

You are in good company, friend, and you are definitely not alone. Joy is at hand! It begins HERE. It begins NOW. With the new mindset you'll gain while reading this book and working on yourself, you'll find that the journey IS the destination.

The adventure of joy and happiness begins today.

God Bless.

—**Nicholas Vescovi**

INTRODUCTION

What is "Happiness"?

Happiness is the one thing all people wish for but few people ever seem to achieve.

Everybody thinks money will buy the happiness they're looking for, but money isn't the key to happiness.

Now, don't get me wrong. Money helps. With money, you don't find yourself stressing out about where your next meal is coming from. You don't worry about how you can't pay your rent. You don't wonder if you're going to end up living on the street—again.

Money buys busy people more time and freedom, but what money doesn't buy is happiness. Think about it. If money was the key to happiness, then why do so many celebrities commit suicide? These are people who seem to have it all—houses, cars, money, fame—but all that stuff isn't enough.

Unfortunately, time and freedom also give people who are already unhappy even more time to sit and stew about their unhappiness. They may not be worried about money, but they have nine gazillion other thoughts running through their heads.

Have you ever thought to yourself (or said out loud), "I'll be happy when ..."?

I'll be happy when ...

I get that dream house ...

Or that dream car ...

Or my perfect partner ...

Or when I accomplish this big goal of mine ...

Then I will *finally* be happy ...

Those four words became a curse over my life.

And this book is the story of how that curse was finally broken.

CHAPTER ONE

Scared to Death and Doomed at Seven

I was born the youngest of four into a good ol' fashioned midwestern family on a beautiful spring day. Granted, it was May in Wisconsin, so there may have been snow on the ground, and it was probably cold AF, but life seemed to be good, right?

That's what everyone pretended, but the skeletons eventually fell out of the closet.

By the time I was five, my parents had divorced. Shit kinda went downhill fast from there. Dad moved a couple of hours away, and Mom was left to raise us. Well, as you may have figured out, with a single mom trying to raise four kids on her own, my older sisters ended up watching over us a lot of the time.

My mom was a wonderful woman, and I believe she tried her best, but we bounced from place to place every six months or so, never settling down in one place for more than a year.

I realized later that it was because we could never afford to pay the rent. To give you a frame of reference, I ended up going to 15 different schools in 12 years.

Now, before you think I'm just trying to paint a picture of "poor me," I want you to know that I have absolutely no animosity toward anyone and am thankful for my upbringing because I would not be the man I am today without the life I've lived.

I simply want you to understand the programming I had. Most people will do exactly as their parents did. You can't fault someone for doing what they never knew was wrong.

So, for years, we bounced from place to place. I remember when I was seven years old, my mom's alcoholic boyfriend at the time would beat the shit out of her every night. I wanted nothing more than to be somewhere else. Anywhere else. I would cry myself to sleep at night and wish for a different life.

That's when I started delaying my happiness with those four dreaded words:

"I'll be happy when ..."

Things eventually got so bad that my brother and sisters and I moved back in with my dad, but four kids is a lot to handle.

Just like I hold no hard feelings against my mom, I hold none against my father. He was the oldest boy of nine kids on a farm. He wasn't allowed to show emotion, and his family worked him nonstop. Changing his programming wasn't even a question. He lived life the only way he knew how.

My dad wasn't around much (he worked a ton, which is all he ever knew, and he still does to this day), so my two older sisters and my older brother looked after me. They made sure I had the essentials, including meals.

As the time came for my sisters to move away and start their separate lives, it was just my brother and me, and my brother always made sure I was taken care of. I'll always be thankful to him for watching over me.

At nine years old, I started detailing cars at a dealership, ingrained with the same insane work ethic I saw in my Dad. I worked there every night, from after school until midnight. I had more cash than any 9-year-old needed, but it was empowering, and I felt it.

While this work ethic would be a great asset, it would also prove to be a downfall, as you will soon see.

When I was around 11 and my brother was between 15 and 16, I made a choice to change my life.

During this time, my mother had been in and out of jail and eventually made her way to Orange County, California. One summer, I went to visit her and decided I wanted to go and live with her. My dad just let me go. I packed my things in a couple of boxes and boarded a plane from cold AF Wisconsin to sunny SoCal.

When I first got there, it seemed like my mom had finally changed. She was smiling and happy and seemed like she had gotten her mind right. I started school out there and immediately loved it.

Life was good for a while, and it seemed as though my mom had finally found her happiness. It didn't last long, though.

We soon went down the same difficult path of being kicked out of place after place. At one point, we even lived in a shady hotel room.

We eventually found a room to rent in a lower-income area of town— a single room in a cockroach-infested house. If you put your food down, the cockroaches would have carried it away.

Honestly, though, none of that mattered to me—for one reason. I felt loved. I know this may sound weird, but I knew my mom loved me. Even in the shittiest of places, we found a way to be happy.

At Universal Studios, posing with my mom.

Years went by, and eventually, an old boyfriend of my mom's showed up. He was a truck driver from Florida, and they would talk and hang out when he was in town. He managed to convince her to leave California and move to Florida with him.

I wasn't happy about the move, but I was only 17, so I ended up moving from Orange County, Southern California, to the Middle of Fucking Nowhere, Northern Florida.

Things went OK for a while (other than the huge-ass spiders and the rattlesnakes), but history seems to repeat itself, and as you might expect, they broke up. There we were again: homeless and living out of a hotel room.

Do you see the pattern?

We would do really well for a bit and then fall back down into the depths of shit over and over again. Not only did I do this as a kid with my mom, but I also ended up repeating this pattern in my life as an adult.

I'm pointing this out now because I want you to get this:

History will repeat itself for you, too, unless you make some very intentional changes.

These changes have nothing to do with your temporary outer world.

They have everything to do with your complex inner world.

You've got to change how your mind thinks and processes your outer world into your inner world.

You probably know what I'm talking about, even if you're not wandering from one hellhole to the next. The shit you're in—whatever it is—keeps repeating. You keep falling into the same pattern, am I right?

All right, back to the story ... I finally graduated high school in Florida, and I graduated with honors. I finished my senior year as a home-schooler because I had constant migraines from a condition called Chiari Malformation Type 1. Basically, my brain is too big to fit in my skull, and it grew down my spine, pinching it and causing migraine headaches. ("Look at the big brain on Jared—he sounds so smart!" Yeah, yeah. If you haven't noticed, I'm more of a smart *ass*.)

I wasn't interested in college because I had no clue what I wanted to do, so I went to work. I worked for a little Baskin Robbins ice cream shop in Valdosta, Georgia, where my mom finally found a trailer to rent.

My dad had instilled in me what his dad instilled in him—the ridiculous work ethic I mentioned—so I was quickly promoted to manager. In this role, I went through corporate management training.

This is where I first got my taste of the business world. I was a quick learner, and as I turned this failing business into a profitable business, I got some of the best hands-on business education available. I may have done too good of a job, though.

After I turned the business around, it was sold to a new owner. As I was only 19 years old at the time, the new owners decided I wasn't essential, so I was let go.

So, I went to work at Wal-Mart. Working my ass off, making my way up the chain, I worked third shift. This is where I would spend a good portion of my time as an adult. I've always felt the darkness and solitude of night calming and peaceful.

As mom continued in her struggles, I helped keep a roof over our heads and food on the table. Soon, I grew tired of Georgia and decided to move back to Wisconsin where I was born and where my brother, two sisters, and dad all lived fairly close together, near Madison.

My mom stubbornly agreed to move back with me, and I rented an apartment for the two of us. Almost immediately, I landed a job as a manager of a Target store in Madison.

It was an odd time.

I hadn't seen or talked to my dad much since I left for California eleven years prior, but we tried to make up for lost time. I continued to work at Target for a year or so until I met a woman named Sara, who was also an employee at Target.

She hated me at first, but once we got to know each other, we became inseparable.

She turned into the best friend I never had.

Moving so much early in life, I never made any real long-term friends. It's hard to make lasting relationships when you don't live in one area for more than six months at a time. The benefit of moving around so much, though, is that I learned early on how to instantly be comfortable talking to random people.

Young and naive Jared and Sara

I soon realized the situation with Sara wasn't going to work for long. Being her boss and being something beyond just a friend after a while made continuing to work at Target impossible.

Sara or Target? Hmmm. It wasn't really much of a choice: I left Target and kept Sara. Coca-Cola® took me on as a merchandiser, filling stores' shelves across the state.

Things blossomed between us, and I was soon presented with a much more difficult choice than my decision to leave Target. Do I keep supporting my mom, or do I move on and into the life I wanted to share with Sara?

Sara meant so much to me, I knew I had to start a life with her. She was the first person I ever fully trusted. I never really trusted my parents, and I never really had any real friends.

I was the guy who everyone thought had a million friends because I was good at making people laugh—but making people laugh is different from real relationships or friendships.

I never let anyone truly see me, know my past, or be part of my life.

My mom was still stuck in her up/down cycle, and even though I had supported her most of my life, I knew it was time for me to be on my own.

Sara and I moved in together, and life was pretty good—for a while.

I left Coca-Cola when I was scouted by Red Bull® for a sales job, thanks to my reputation and work ethic. I learned a lot of valuable lessons in that job, including how to talk to prospects and negotiate contracts. I gained experience in sales and marketing. I traveled all over Wisconsin.

The only problem was that I worked super long hours and wasn't paid shit. I was always number one or number two salesman for the two years I was there, but when I asked for commission, they refused. I found a manufacturing job that paid way more, put in my notice, and moved on.

Things with Sara were going great. But, I had gotten used to moving every few months and starting over, and I had a bit of trepidation about getting married. Ok, I'll say it. I had some serious commitment issues.

It was especially frustrating because that Beyoncé song "Single Ladies" with the lyric, "If you liked it, then you shoulda put a ring on it" was everywhere on the radio. Sara would shake her finger and laugh when we heard it. I knew she was only partially joking.

At this point, we had been dating for four years. I finally worked through some of my commitment issues and bought a ring ... but not without playing one last joke.

Early on in our relationship, I had bought Sara a pair of peridot earrings and a necklace. They were her favorite. Unfortunately, though, Sara ended up losing one of her earrings in a severe car accident. Someone came up the wrong side of the road and hit her head-on.

Honestly, I will never forget that day.

We both worked for Coca-Cola. We had just finished at a store, and she called me as we were both driving to the next store. Shortly after we got on the phone, I heard the collision.

While still on the phone, all I could hear was her screaming in agony, and I heard her say, "I can't feel my legs." Then, the call dropped, and she did not answer when I tried calling her back.

I immediately called 911 and raced to her approximate location. I followed the fire trucks and ambulances and was one of the first ones on the scene. Sara got hurt, but luckily she recovered.

To this day, I still won't talk to her on the phone while she is driving.

In this crash, her earrings went from a pair to a single. It was not found, even after searching her wrecked car in the junkyard. I knew those earrings had a special place in her heart.

Sara knew something was up. I had received a package, but I was very secretive about what was inside. On the day I had decided to propose, I hid two jewelry boxes. I called her downstairs, got down on one knee, and showed her the first box. I could tell by the look on her face that she knew exactly what was happening.

She was overjoyed.

But there was a catch. When she opened the first box, she found a pair of the same peridot earrings she had lost in the accident.

Honestly, the look on her face was priceless.

She was so prepared to say yes, but she found no ring inside. She was overjoyed at the thought of me buying her those same earrings—but we both know that's not what she really wanted.

I'm not cruel, though. I only paused for a second as I reached into my other pocket and pulled out an engagement ring.

I asked her to marry me.

Of course, she said yes. She burst into tears, then laughter, and she may or may not have punched me—it depends on who's telling the story. It's a moment that we will both never forget.

Sara and I are fairly simple people. We were planning on skipping the big wedding and just going to Vegas to tie the knot. My aunt, though, gave us the offer of a lifetime: the perfect wedding venue—her house in Malibu California, overlooking the ocean.

On our wedding day in Malibu, California.

We had a beautiful wedding surrounded by close family and friends, but it wasn't without its hiccups. Looking back, I realize this was one of my first big signs that I didn't know how to properly handle stress or my emotions. I held them all in which would cause some severe health problems.

Two days before the wedding, my back locked up and completely gave out. I was hunched over to one side and in the most pain I've ever felt. It wasn't like I was doing anything crazy. I was pulling my swimming trunks off after a dip in the pool.

Those two days leading up to the wedding were filled with doctor and chiropractor appointments. Thankfully, I was able to walk down the aisle to see my beautiful bride standing there.

We had a beautiful wedding and an amazing time in California. We road-tripped out there in our Jeep®, and it was the first time Sara had seen the western half of the U.S. or the Pacific Ocean.

Our first Jeep® on Pismo Beach Sand Dunes on our way to our wedding.

We had an awesome trip back to Wisconsin, driving through Utah and Colorado before returning home.

Shortly after we returned, Sara became pregnant with our first son, Sebastian, wo we started looking for a house. My dad had a crazy girlfriend who offered to "rent to own" her house to us, which was in rough shape. It was through that experience that I learned the important lesson of putting things in writing.

Not long after we invested over $20,000 into fixing and remodeling the whole house, she kicked us out. In short, she saw how great it looked and changed her mind about selling it to us. My dad took her side, and I was left struggling to find a place for my family.

Once again, I was homeless—this time, with a wife who was pregnant.

Sara and I did find a place. It was a brand-new house, a little out of the way, but perfect for us. We weren't homeowners, but it was the house where we brought our baby boy home from the hospital, and we were happy.

Sebastian was a joker from the start and has grown into an amazing person. He came into this world on April first (April Fools' Day). The fact that it was three weeks before Sara's due date made people think we were playing some elaborate April Fools' joke.

I've always had that sense of humor to make people laugh, so people didn't put it past me. I wasn't joking though, and people eventually believed me after I sent some photos of Sara in the hospital bed. It was a long day, but thankfully we ended up with a healthy baby boy, our April Fools' baby.

Life was going great, but it wasn't without its challenges. Fourteen months after Sebastian was born, we welcomed our second son into the world. Isaac was born with clubfeet, so he had to have surgery after surgery. He was in casts most of the first year of his life, and once out of the casts, he had to be in a mechanism very similar to a snowboard. His feet were strapped in at all times, keeping them pointed out. He did turn out to be a hell of a snowboarder later in life, quickly picking it up.

About a month after Isaac was born, I got a call that would shift my entire life.

I remember it like it was yesterday.

I was at work when my sister called me. She said she found my mom dead in her apartment.

I rushed over there to find my sister in tears. My other sister, my brother, and I were all in shock.

For as long as I can remember, my mom struggled with her own demons. At age 56, my mom passed away from an accidental overdose on painkillers.

My world was turned upside down. My mom suddenly passed away, my son was born with serious health issues, and my family was about to lose the only house I had ever really been happy in. I started to crack.

I had no idea how to handle the emotions that were going through my body. Have you ever seen the movie *Tommy Boy*? The part where he talks about yanking the steering wheel and crashing his car into a bridge? That was me, every day on my way to work. I had no idea how to deal with the pain I was going through.

I was severely depressed, working a job I hated, $500,000 in debt from my son's surgeries, and about to find myself homeless again. (Patterns are a bitch, aren't they?) I was in a dark place.

We rented this brand new house during the housing crash, but once the market improved, the developers started selling all their houses, including ours. Unfortunately, we couldn't purchase it because of the mountain of medical debt we were in, and our credit was trashed.

It was around this time that I met someone. A mentor, you might say. This person was about to show me how to bust open that trap of repeated behavior I've mentioned.

He was about to show me how to change my life.

CHAPTER TWO

The Point of No Return

It was a morning just like any other weekday morning. I was depressed, overweight, and struggling to find the energy to just get up and go to work.

I was scrolling Facebook™ in bed, and that's when it happened …

The moment that changed my life.

One of my buddies, Andy, had shared a post by a guy named Sean Whalen. As I looked more closely at the picture, I realized it featured a photo of Sean and the baby he had with his ex-wife.

Something about this photo intrigued me. He was being so open about his problems, his demons, and his life.

In my world, everyone hid that shit behind a mask and put on a pretty façade—something I'd been conditioned to do and had been doing my whole life.

I sat up and started reading every post that Sean had written on Facebook about flipping houses (something I had always wanted to do, but never got much past reading all the books on it), about his life, and about this thing he was doing at the time called "Wake Up Warrior."

What hit me hardest was his 100% accountability for his actions and his 100% honesty.

As I dug deeper, watching videos and reading posts from both Sean Whalen and Garrett J. White, the founder of Wake Up Warrior, something shifted inside me.

The pattern was disrupted. I don't know how to explain it, but from that day forward, instead of blaming everything that happened to me on something outside of my control, I started to really own my shit— good, bad, or indifferent.

Patterns dictate much of what we do.

A great deal of what happens in our lives are not things we even consciously think about. We all do thousands of things every day without ever thinking about them. Take breathing, for instance. We do it all day, but unless we intentionally focus on it, we do it without thinking.

Without realizing it, people pick up a lot of their habits from their parents—from birth to childhood and into adulthood.

I am no different from you. I picked up both good things and bad, just like anyone else.

As you can see from my story so far, I've struggled with breaking those bad habits. They are deeply ingrained, and sometimes it takes a lot for the pattern to be broken.

The good thing, though, is that reading this book and hearing my story will help you recognize the patterns you may not see in your own life. In the second part of the book, I will give you some ways to begin making changes—a process that is essential if you want to define your own happiness.

Something inside me changed, and it was reflected on the outside, too.

The first change I made was our living situation. The only place I could afford to rent was a shit box of a 150-year-old house that was maybe 700 square feet. Two bedrooms and a floor that felt like you might fall through it. It didn't even have a basement. It was built on boulders, and they were crumbling underneath the house.

It was a hell of a change from the brand new, three-bedroom house we had been living in, but at least we could afford it. And because it was a shit hole, our crappy credit from all the medical bills wasn't an issue.

I mean, no one else wanted to live there. Why not us, right?

This was Step 1 in taking 100% accountability for my life with zero excuses.

Thanks to another mentor I discovered—a man named Jesse Elder, who was a mentor and friend to Sean and Garrett—I was introduced to the 1% shift. His advice is to shift your life one percent each day, and in one year, you will live in a totally different world.

What is the One Percent Shift? Exactly what it sounds like. Shift your thoughts, your actions, your habits one percent each day. Your goal is to be 1% better than you were yesterday. That's it.

Your goal is not to make a 180-degree shift overnight. Why is this important? Because shifting slowly gives you time to adjust to every little change without bombarding your body and your mind.

When you try to pull a 180 overnight, your body will go into survival mode to protect itself from too much change at once. It wants to preserve its status quo.

My entire life, I've struggled with my weight. I love food and a bit of drink. I am a fairly large man at 6'4" and my weight would constantly sway from super fit at 200 pounds to unfit at 340 pounds.

I would get so sick and tired of being fat and energy-less that I would try to make a radical shift. I'd starve myself, work out, and lose a ton of weight, only to be back where I was before, six months down the road. Sound familiar?

Learning about and implementing the One Percent Shift changed my entire life. No longer was I batting for the fence, trying to hit home runs. I was simply swinging singles every day, getting better, bit by bit—physically, mentally, and emotionally.

How does this look in real life? Let's use a health example because I think everyone can relate to it. The old me would try to make massive shifts in my diet. I'd start intense exercise programs, and I'd eventually give up and resort back to my old habits. The approach for me that finally stuck was the 1% shift.

Instead of a massive diet and exercise shift, I simply tried to eat 1% better than I did yesterday. Instead of a carb-loaded meal at night, I would start by adding a side salad. In the next few days, I would keep reducing the amount of carbs until I was only eating veggies or a salad with my dinner.

As I slowly started to eat better, I started having more energy. I didn't make a huge change, like going to the gym every day. I simply aimed to be 1% better than yesterday. I would take the dog for a walk at night instead of watching TV. Again, a small shift that wouldn't leave me regretting it the next morning.

As I started to slowly get more active, I felt better and better. So I would continue down this path of 1% better every day. I'd add in pushups. Then squats. Then a full workout three times a week. Eventually, I got up every single morning and worked out.

Can you see the difference? One is a massive shift that throws your body and mind into panic mode for survival. The other is shifting 1% better each day (kinda like evolution), giving your mind and body time to adjust, create new habits, and evolve without tripping the survival sensors to take over.

I used physical health in these examples, as I think it is the easiest to relate to, but as you might imagine, this will work in every area of your life—physically, mentally, and financially. Try it for yourself. Keep a journal and write down every night or morning how you were 1% better today than you were yesterday.

This will create massive confidence, happiness, and momentum in your life. It will get you through those difficult times and give you something to build off of each day.

You will see in the next chapter the start of my turnaround. What may seem like an overnight change was actually me deciding to be 1% better each day. This creates an amazing thing called momentum, and once you have some momentum, it feels like nothing can slow you down.

Thanks to Jesse Elder, I had decided to make small, 1% shifts in my life with the hope of creating big results in one year.

At the time, I worked in a factory. Since I couldn't afford to go to the gym, I worked out at work. Whenever I had a spare moment or while I was on break, I would do pushups or squats.

21

I used the tools around me. If I found a piece of metal that was heavy, I would do some sort of exercise with it to make my muscles move.

This shit worked. I was feeling better and losing weight.

My next step was getting control over my finances.

There was no way for my wife and me to keep up with the medical bills, so we filed for bankruptcy. It was one of the hardest things I've ever done. Since I regard honor and integrity as core values to live by, I viewed declaring bankruptcy as something less than honorable. But it was the one action I saw I could do to break the pattern, to get us back on our feet.

My job at the factory wasn't the greatest, but I was a sponge for knowledge and learned everything I could about the entire manufacturing process while I was there.

I moved from the start of the production line to the end, wrapping the product and shipping it out of the warehouse. Then, I went into the physical testing lab. We would test all the vinyl and products to make sure they were within certain specifications and also develop new products.

Honestly, I knew this wasn't what I wanted to spend the rest of my life doing, but I was still a sponge for knowledge. Being a sponge paid extreme dividends later on in life when I went into the business of creating physical products. Knowing the entire manufacturing process from start to out-the-door-and-shipped gave me a huge advantage.

No matter where you work now, it could be less than ideal. Hell, I hated this job with a passion, but because I went in every day and did my best and kept learning, it set me up for bigger things down the road. Every skill I learned at every job has helped me succeed in my own business.

When I was working in the lab downstairs, I decided to learn something that always interested me, which was real estate.

As soon as I knew the direction I wanted to take, I took action. I saved up the money to get my books and take the online class to get my real estate license. I used every free moment I had to study and go through the course.

Every work break and lunch break, I was studying. I even studied during work sometimes (hehe). I had downtime working in the lab, and instead of slacking off like most employees, I worked my butt off to get my daily tasks for my job done and spent all the remaining time working on myself and my education.

Sara and I decided to work opposite shifts so we didn't have to pay for childcare for our two young boys. I worked the second shift at the warehouse, not getting home till 11:30 PM. I studied until 3 AM, slept a couple of hours, then got up at 5 AM to take care of the boys so Sara could head off to the hospital where she worked as a nurse. No excuses.

And you know what? I took the real estate exam after a couple months of diligently studying and got my license.

I felt on top of the world!

I was starting to get healthier, mentally and physically. Financially, I was handling my shit and getting on top of my finances. That alone gave me confidence out the ass. Things were going great!

That's what I wanted to believe.

The truth was, though, I was struggling.

I had built a life I had come to hate.

I was putting in 80+ hour weeks trying to grow my real estate business while still working a full-time job that I hated. I never even had time to see my own family. I used to talk to my kids using FaceTime at dinner because I wasn't home to be with them.

My inner voice was telling me this whole time to quit the job I hated and to jump head-first into being an entrepreneur, but my brain wouldn't let me do it.

It's a hard battle to follow your heart instead of your brain.

Logic is telling you to stay in the safe job—even if you are miserable. Your brain tells you it's too risky to start your own business.

I didn't listen to my heart for the longest time, and then I wound up in a hospital bed because of the inner struggle I was dealing with. My body was trying to tell me to follow my heart, but my brain wouldn't let me.

When I didn't listen to this voice inside me, I'd start experiencing back pain. I had never learned to deal with my emotions, and all that stress would plant itself in my body and in my back.

I told myself, even promised myself, that I would leave my factory job and my back would start to feel better.

As I continued to work the job I hated, my back continued to get worse. It was like my body was trying to cripple me to follow my heart, but I'm stubborn and wouldn't listen. I did a vicious cycle of physical therapy, chiropractic appointments, injections, and whatever else doctors could do to try to help me. This cycle went on for over a year— a year of pain and agony searching for answers …

Until one morning, I woke up and couldn't walk.

I couldn't feel my left leg. The nerves were completely pinched off. All I remember is dragging my body with my arms to my kids' room. Somehow, I was able to pull myself off the floor, pick up my crying son out of his crib, and call my wife at work.

After that, I blacked out from the pain.

Sara carried me to the car and hauled me to the emergency room.

To give you an idea of her strength, I weighed 250 pounds at 6'4" and she's 5'2" and 120 pounds.

After we got to the hospital and I received some pain meds, I was rushed into an MRI. The doctor came in and gave me two choices: either have emergency back surgery or never walk again. Hard call, right? The nerve down my left leg was severely pinched by a herniation in my spine. So off I went to the operating room, not knowing if I was ever going to be able to walk again.

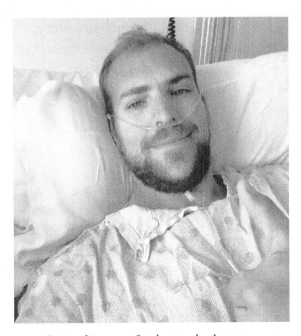

Just waking up after having back surgery.

Oddly enough, when I woke up from surgery, my mind was completely clear and at ease. I knew I could never go back to that life—the life I hated but felt powerless to change.

The thought of never being able to play with my kids again if I continued down that path was enough for me to promise myself that this time I would not only listen to my inner voice but I would also do what it said.

We all have that voice inside our heads. It's the one that tries to get us to step out of our comfort zones and try something new.

It says to stop caring what everyone else thinks and just jump.

Do something you love doing.

I want to encourage you to pay attention to that voice. If I had listened to it earlier, I probably wouldn't have ended up in the hospital.

Truth be told, I'm grateful that I wound up on that operating table because it finally pushed me to leave the job I hated. Even if I wanted to go back to work, I couldn't physically do anything. It broke the cycle of me not allowing myself to follow my dreams. I had no other options. Now, I had to believe in myself.

Cycles don't break easily, though, and the road to recovery wasn't easy either.

So here I was at 30 years old, unable to walk or even wipe my own ass. I couldn't drive for four months, and for another six months after that, I had to use a cane because the nerve down my leg was pinched so badly that I would fall if I didn't have something to lean on.

I had what doctors call severe drop foot. In essence, I was unable to control my leg, and it would drop, and I would fall.

The surgery saved the nerve from being completely pinched off and prevented me from losing the ability to walk. But it wasn't an instant fix.

Even the doctors said I might never walk normally again.

Determined to walk normally again, I threw away my walker after four months. I walked to my back yard with a machete and cut a tree branch off a maple tree and created my own cane. Here I am, pictured taking my very young boys, Sebastian and Isaac, for a walk through the woods with the cane I created.

It wasn't just a physical blow. It was a mental blow.

You see, my entire life, I have been the strong one, both mentally and physically. This setback almost broke me. All the confidence I had built was gone.

Everyone could see how broken I was physically, but the only person who knew what had happened to me on the inside was Sara. No one knew of my inner turmoil other than her.

Of course, everyone could see the outer pain—the effects of the surgery and not being able to walk—but to be honest, that was the easy part.

I felt broken. Not just physically this time but also emotionally. I had done everything right, but everything felt wrong.

I struggled for a long time, trying to figure out who the fuck I had pissed off to get here.

I did the things every guru at the time was saying to do.

I had success at my fingertips, and it all came crashing down around me.

Not only was I broke again from being out of work for a year, but I had just filed bankruptcy the year before and had started turning my credit—and my life—around. Now, I was in debt again from my back surgery.

I had changed my life, improved my health, taken 100% responsibility for my actions, and, still, here I was, back at square one: broke, both physically and financially, and on the verge of spontaneous combustion.

Life has a funny way of testing you sometimes.

How much do you really want something?

Are you truly committed to improving your life and breaking the cycle?

It's like life was saying, *"Let me see if you can still keep going after I take away your ability to walk and smash your face into the dirt."*

If you can't see by now, I carried my mom's same old patterns with me. I would blaze a trail and do fucking awesome, and then I would burn it all to the ground around me.

It took a very long time for me to figure this out, but it all stemmed from a feeling of lack—from feeling like I didn't deserve anything I created.

I worked my ass to the bone to create amazing things, and when I got what I wanted ("I'll be happy when …"), I would throw it all away, not feeling like I deserved it.

That is what I am here to address: why people cannot be happy, physically and mentally.

I'm not talking about people who everyone knows are unhappy. I'm talking about the people like me who put on a happy face, have a sense of humor, and will always make you smile (for example, Robin Williams), but deep down inside won't allow themselves to be happy or feel successful no matter what they accomplish.

They may have a great life, a great family, and everyone thinks they have all their shit together, but deep down … no matter what shiny face they put on, no matter how many people they can make laugh, no matter how much material shit they accumulate … it's not enough.

They still won't allow themselves to be happy.

At her core, my mom didn't believe she deserved happiness, and neither did I.

CHAPTER THREE

The Great Turnaround

My turnaround started with almost becoming homeless again.

The house we lived in (the shitbox) should have been condemned, but it wasn't. For one reason. The owner was a big real estate developer in that town, and he was slowly putting the property pieces of the puzzle together so he could own several blocks right near downtown, which was prime redevelopment land.

Once we found out, we got the fuck out, before he got his permits together and decided to tear everything down, leaving us homeless.

These fucking patterns, man.

Sara and I set out to find a new place to live. We found a 3-bedroom house on a 37-acre apple orchard. We could hardly believe it, but the rent at this amazing place was the same as our tiny, little shitbox!

I was out of work, still recovering from back surgery, but we went for it, not even knowing if we could pay for it. It felt right, like we were chosen to live there.

This would turn out to be the best thing we ever did. Not only was this a great house but it was also surrounded by multi-million dollar homes. Really, we had no close neighbors because of all the land, but our two nearest neighbors lived in 10,000 and 16,000 square-foot homes.

Don't underestimate the power of those you allow in your life and the people you surround yourself with.

So we moved to this cozy home, nestled on dozens of acres of land, surrounded by affluent people, and we all lived "happily ever after," right?

Wrong.

After my back surgery, I spiraled into the depths of despair and depression. I became a small fraction of the man I had become. All the self-improvement I had done and everything I had learned over the years went straight out the window.

You would think all that training with daily implementation would come right back, but it didn't. My mind was in a dark place, and I was back to being the same pragmatic asshole stuck in his own head, unable to break free.

Looking back now, it's hard to comprehend everything I went through leading up to my surgery. I had completely transformed my life, my being, my entire mental processing. And I instantly fell back down, somehow forgetting it all.

I spent a long time after my surgery just trying to figure out who I was. I had changed so much in just a few short years, but my momentum seemed to be instantly immobilized once I hit that surgery table. There were ups and downs physically, but I was fighting the biggest battle inside my head.

I had to make a conscious choice to find and become the real me—the me that I was deep inside, who had the courage to decide enough is enough.

There was no instant improvement. It was a long, drawn-out process.

How could I fall so far back down the rabbit hole after soaring out of it?

One night, I finally found myself completely fed up with my current situation. I made the choice to change my life again. To find me again. To find the confident, conquering man I once was.

I took a mental trip back in time—not to bury myself in pity but to figure out where I went wrong and where I went right.

I started all over again with my self-improvement. I went back to reading, then training myself in the same things that originally pulled me out of this hole to begin with.

I went back to my mentors—the people I followed online. One in particular, Jesse Elder, helped me figure out how to conquer this mind of mine. Through Jesse, I found Ryan Daniel Moran and his YouTube video called "Zero To $1M on Amazon in 12 months."

I now had a new mentor, one who would go on to change my entire world, but I had to make a choice. Did I want this? Was I going to have it?

You're damn fucking right I was going to have it!

Through him, all of my previous training and action to get here came back, flowing through my veins.

I was alive again.

The old Jared had died many times but kept reviving himself like a zombie. I'd kill that fucker off, but he just kept coming back. He may as well have been a fucking cat with his nine lives.

I was ready to live a life by design, not by whatever was thrown at me.

A lot of people look at my life now and seem to think my success happened by accident or that it was luck, but my journals from that time in my life tell another story.

I had designed my life to a T, writing out exactly what I wanted and what I would be doing. I worked my way forward by designing backward.

So, I had two aces in my hand: finally learning how to control my mind and an unbelievable work ethic.

None of this would have been possible without Sara's 100% support. She has always been my #1 cheerleader, constantly pushing me to follow my dreams. Whenever I would get stuck in my own head, she would set me straight. She would ask me what I wanted, and when I would tell her, she would say, "OK. Then, GO FUCKING DO IT."

So, I developed a plan. Well, actually, Ryan developed the plan. I just followed that shit to a T. I committed to success, and no matter what, I would not quit. I would step out of my comfort zone and become the person I was always meant to be.

My goal was to go from zero to a million dollars in a year. Well, right at that moment, I was technically below zero because we were massively in debt, and we could barely feed our family or pay our bills.

I would use what was ingrained in me as a child to my benefit. I had zero money, but I was ready to outwork any motherfucker out there! Not accomplishing my goal was not an option.

I began by doing anything I could to start the income flowing again. It happens that I have some woodworking skills and tools, so I did anything and everything I could to keep the lights on and start chipping away at our debt.

Need something fixed? Here I am. Got something you need built? I'll get my tools and be right over.

You have to remember I was still physically recovering from surgery. Most days my body hated me, but I refused to give up.

I must have built hundreds of these Adirondack chairs
to keep a roof over our heads and food on the table.

That kind of work might be admirable and all, but it wasn't the real game plan. It was just a way of keeping us from digging even further into debt.

The problem with implementing Ryan's plan was that I had no money to start.

I needed money to develop a product and create a brand. I scoured the internet and found a new thing (new to me) called retail arbitrage. Basically, I would spend my days at thrift stores and any big box store, scouring the shelves for deals I could flip on Amazon.

I started with books. I read a lot and knew books, so I went to Goodwill with $20 and bought 20 books for $1 each and listed them on Amazon. I came out with $50 to $100. I repeated this process over and over again for months, hell-bent on making my goal of one million in one year.

My gains began to add up. While I was flipping books, I was also learning everything I could about how to develop a brand and build a website, all while taking care of two toddler boys every day. And if you think I'm some sort of e-commerce or computer wizard, think again.

I had almost no skills in the online world, but I got very good at using Google and YouTube to figure shit out.

Eventually, I made enough money to bulk order my first personally-branded product that I created. It was a small, silicone, collapsible bowl for dogs to be able to easily give them water while traveling. I was on top of the world. I finally had this shit figured out!

Sara and I holding our first product that I developed—
a silicone, collapsible dog bowl. It went on to become an Amazon Bestseller.

Yeah, not quite.

My first product basically flopped.

It sold well and became an Amazon bestseller, but it was such a cheap product to sell that I made less than a dollar on each unit sold. That's a lot of fucking units to sell to reach my goal of one million dollars.

The business was bleeding money instead of generating it. But, I kept going and going.

Quitting was not an option.

I pushed on, testing and researching until I finally found something— something I was absolutely convinced would finally launch this business and make some actual fucking money.

And where did I find it? In a fucking Facebook video someone forwarded to me.

CHAPTER FOUR

Open Your Eyes to
What's Right In Front of You

My aunt in California has always been kind of like a second mom to me. When I was a kid, my mom and I would take the drive up from Orange County to Malibu to see her and my cousin.

Later, she would send me cool things she found online, and I always appreciated it because she was a businesswoman herself.

So, one day, she sent me a Facebook video for a product, and I noticed it had a couple hundred thousand views. I knew in an instant it was a real opportunity.

You can call it a hunch, but to me, it was a certainty. All it needed was the right advertising to the right audience, and it would go viral.

It was September, so I was thinking ahead to people shopping online for Christmas.

With no time to lose, I jumped on that shit. Fast. Within hours, I found a supplier. I placed an order and then got some pictures and a listing on my site. I created a video to push on Facebook, and guess what happened . . .

Nothing.

That's right.

Nothing happened.

Didn't see that coming, did you?

Yeah, it's not always as easy as people think, but I pushed on, knowing this opportunity could finally get my family back on our feet.

I narrowed down my target audience. I tested my ads. I tested some more. I kept at it until, bam, that shit went gangbusters.

The next month, October, we hit $80,000 in sales, and in November, we sold almost $200,000 worth of products.

In December, we did another $80,000 in sales and could have done much more, but we sold everything we had in stock. I was even able to take some of the money and begin testing new products to offer.

My tiny office in the basement of our house. It was more of a storage unit in those days—fulfilling/shipping—with boxes of product everywhere.

Now, if my aunt hadn't sent me that video, none of this would've happened. I want to mention her again because I firmly believe that people are the most valuable resource you have, as you'll see soon enough when the shit hits the fan.

The confidence I gained from feeling like I had accomplished something in my life propelled me forward to try those other products and generate that revenue. It took almost six months of diligently working before I got my first break, but after I did, I was all in.

Early on, with that first product, I had to order small quantities (at a higher price) because my supplier was running low on stock of my product.

So I had two choices:

1) Stop selling it even though it was selling well (stay small as a business), or:

2) Continue to sell by finding a manufacturer and placing a bulk order (put on my big-boy panties, bet all my money on this product continuing to sell, and grow my business).

I chose Option 2.

I had to go to the bank and wire $12,000 to China with implicit trust because once I wired the money overseas, it was gone. This was only 30% of the cost, too. They were just finishing up another run, and in a week, I would have to wire the remaining $28,000.

Of course, I verified the supplier as much as I could, but I was still sending $40,000 overseas, and if they fucked me, it would destroy my ass.

I remember driving to the bank, my stomach in knots. I felt like I was going to pass out. I could barely breathe. I remember talking to my mom (who had passed away), looking for some assurance that this was going to be OK. I heard a voice. It said, "Jared, go for it. It will be OK. I'm proud of you. You can do this." I broke down in tears, almost crashing off the road.

I followed my heart, calmed my mind, and sent the money.

Not that long ago, $40,000 was almost a year's worth of pay, and now I was wiring that amount overseas. I patiently waited for the reply of the supplier after sending them the wire transfer confirmation. They said it would ship that night, and they would send tracking numbers.

They sent me the tracking numbers.

The tracking numbers weren't valid.

I almost collapsed.

My heart was beating so fast, I thought it was going to jump out of my chest. I tried to regain my thoughts and stay calm. Then, I remembered what they had told me. The tracking numbers are Fed-Ex tracking numbers, but it will have to be trucked to the airport by a forwarder and then scanned before it gets on a plane to the U.S.

I could do nothing but wait, so that's what I did.

Unable to sleep, I stayed awake for almost two days. I kept checking tracking numbers, hoping and praying I wasn't getting ripped off by my supplier.

Well, the good news is that the 6,000 units were on their way to me. The bad news is that I was selling these so fast that I was now behind on fulfilling almost 1,000 orders before the truck was even unloaded at my door.

I had no time to spare. Instead of sending them to Amazon or another fulfillment center, which would just cost me more time and more money, I decided to "buckle up, Buttercup," and fulfill the orders myself. I ordered all the boxes, tape, and labels before the product arrived so I would be ready.

I had already been awake for 48 hours, printing labels and prepping boxes before the truck finally arrived. It was all hands on deck now. We had orders to fill. With my wife by my side, as well as my two sons (at the time, only 3 and 4 years old), we worked not only as a team but also as a family.

We packed over 1,500 orders over the next 48 hours, worked with the post office, running trucks back and forth, but we got it done.

Keep in mind, I was fulfilling these orders out of my office, which was the basement of our house, in the winter in Wisconsin. It was long, cold work.

I was up for three days straight, and Sara had been up for four straight days because she was also working full-time at the hospital. All the while, we were taking care of two little boys at home.

My sons were all-stars. I have always tried to instill a strong work ethic in them as my father instilled in me, and it showed. For 3- and 4-year olds, they did an amazing job and made me proud. We made a family production line. I would prep the box. Sebastian would put the items in it. Sara would tape it closed, and Isaac would peel and stick the shipping label on it.

They continue to work for me still, today, earning their own money.

Sebastian, now 8, recently bought himself a new bike with money he earned. When my sons want something new, they say, "I want to earn it." You have no idea how proud this makes me!

So, the story of the first few months of success doesn't end there.

We continued to grow and continued to order more products and expand. It wasn't all a gravy train. I slept mostly standing up or in my office chair, catching a few winks when I could.

I placed more orders, and everything was coming in regularly to keep up with demand until we hit a snag. Actually, make that a fucking concrete wall the size of the Hoover Dam.

I had placed one last order before Christmas—my biggest order to date. It was no issue wiring the $100,000 because I had built trust with the supplier at this point. This order should get us through the Christmas season, and I would finally be able to take a nice break (translation: sleep) after the holidays.

Everything was going according to plan. The supplier got the stuff shipped out quicker than expected, and this was good because we were living on borrowed time.

We were out of stock, but we were still taking orders because we knew we had more that should arrive soon and everyone would get their items in plenty of time for Christmas.

That's when we hit the snag.

The items got to Customs in St. Louis and just sat there.

I called and was told there's no problem; this happens from time to time. It should be released by tomorrow.

But it wasn't released. A hundred thousand dollars of supply wasn't moving.

I called again, and then again, and got no answers. A week went by, then almost two.

By now, it was December 13. If I didn't get my supply in the next three days, my customers wouldn't get their purchases by Christmas, and I would be out almost half a million dollars in refunds—money I didn't have because, beyond the cost of inventory, I'd been spending money to keep advertising and promoting these items.

I felt like I was going to have a nervous breakdown. No one was giving me an answer to the question of why Customs wasn't releasing my shipment.

I got on the phone again. I was transferred from one clueless person to another, being put on hold at every step. I could hear my own heart pounding as I waited. My arm was tensing up.

Was I having a heart attack, waiting for someone to pick up a phone on the other end? Was this how it was going to end for me?

A supervisor picked up, finally! She went through what sounded like a script, telling me that there was no reason for a holdup in Customs. It was the busy time of the year, and I'd just have to wait. There was nothing she could do.

My heart sank.

I could barely find the words to speak.

Then I lost my shit. I didn't act like an asshole. I just explained to her that I'd spent $30,000 to have my shipment express air-shipped from

China, and now it's been sitting in Customs for two weeks.

If she didn't have it released and put on a truck to me by tomorrow, I'd be out nearly half a million dollars, which would bankrupt my company.

Then, I told her I was on the verge of a heart attack. I'm sure she could hear my voice trembling and could tell I wasn't blowing smoke up her ass. I really did feel as though I was on the verge of a heart attack.

She paused for a moment, then started the same old script about how she couldn't do anything. Then, she paused again. I think that what I told her finally sank in.

"I'll have it on a truck tonight," she said. "There's no reason for the hold, and I'll make sure it's processed immediately."

I expressed my sincere appreciation for her and then said, "Thank you again." I got off the phone, drenched in sweat, body trembling, clenching my arm ...

And then it hit me.

Even if it shipped that night, I would have to pack and ship over 7,000 orders in one day. That's physically impossible for me to do even with Sara and the boys.

That was when Sara flew into action. I was physically and mentally exhausted, and she simply took up the reins herself.

4 | OPEN YOUR EYES TO WHAT'S RIGHT IN FRONT OF YOU

Back in the days when I was managing a Target store, some of the employees I used to manage were Albanians. They all knew and watched out for each other, and Sara was Facebook friends with a few of them. She reached out and said, "Jared needs a favor."

Even after ten years, they didn't hesitate. Because I had treated them all with respect when I was their boss, they wanted to show up for me when I needed them most.

Word went around, and before I knew it, I had sixteen people ready to show up when my inventory arrived.

Remember earlier when I said that people are the most valuable resource you have?

Well, this is where the shit hits the fan and people show up to help me avoid potentially the biggest mess of my life up to now (and as you know now, I've made a lot of them).

Here's what I was facing. My shipment wouldn't arrive at my house until December 16. And, to get customers their products by Christmas, it had to ship—from my house to theirs—on December 16!

Sara and I stayed up the next two days prepping everything we could. I printed over 7,000 labels and sorted them by color and size so that we could create an assembly line. She and the boys prepared the boxes. And we scheduled a 53-foot USPS semi-trailer to arrive on the evening of the 16th.

At 8:00 on the morning of December 16, sixteen Albanians showed up to work for the entire day (many of them brought their kids, who needed to be looked after). It was December in Wisconsin, meaning it was cold and about to snow. We were working out of our basement and garage, which meant no heat. Everyone had on long coats and gloves. It was surely a sight to see and remember.

We had teams set up, each for a specific type or size of product that needed to be fulfilled. And we all took turns going upstairs to watch the children (and warm up).

At 9:00 AM, the FedEx truck from St. Louis arrived and unloaded its cargo on my gravel driveway. Because it was cold as the north pole out there, we only opened the garage door when we had a full pallet of product to bring in or a full pallet of boxes loaded and ready to ship out.

At 10:00, I got a call from the Postmaster. She told me that a winter storm was rolling in, and she couldn't wait till evening to send the tractor-trailer. She wanted to send it to us now, get it loaded, and have it back on the road as soon as possible.

I begged for more time. I told her I'd fill that entire 53-foot trailer, but the load wouldn't be fully boxed and labeled for hours. She said if we waited too long, they'd be snowed in. The truck wouldn't go anywhere.

Okay, I told her, send it early, but it's not leaving until we've got it filled.

So, we had six hours to pack 7,000 orders.

Everyone worked as a team. The truck showed up at 2:00 PM. We weren't even close to ready, but that big empty trailer was something we now could see. I don't know if it inspired us as much as it terrified us. What I do know is that there was no let-up in our efforts.

There were pallets scattered all over the driveway. We loaded them with labeled boxes, shrink-wrapped them, and laid tarps over each one to protect them from the gathering snow.

The drivers told me they had to get moving. I told them the truck wasn't leaving till we were done. They could tell by my expression that it wasn't negotiable. (Keep in mind, I'm 6'4" and a bit imposing.) The drivers even started pitching in, helping to pack boxes and wrap pallets.

At 5:30 PM, the truck was loaded and on its way, ready to deliver all of those products in time for Christmas. We did it, but just barely.

At that point, I was completely overwhelmed, not just from sleep deprivation, but also from what we just accomplished. I thanked and gave my sincere appreciation to every person there—the people who made it happen. A lot of those people took a day off from their jobs at Target just to help me.

Sara, the boys, and I were supposed to head three hours north that night for my Grandma's Christmas, but our bodies were shot, and with the snow piling up, we decided to leave in the morning instead.

We headed inside and collapsed, having been up for 3 and 4 days straight. We had nothing left in us. We slept well that night.

Now, I want to take a step back for a second and share a little secret.

You know how most people, if they could wish for anything, would wish for money?

Not me. I would wish for the right people with the exact knowledge or help I needed to come into my life at the exact moment I needed them.

Why? Money will come and go, but people will always be the catalyst to launch you to that next level. People who work for you will be the ones who help you achieve your goals.

That brilliant idea for a business? It may come from a person you know.

The product that finally took my business from severe red to profitable? It came from a person who sent it to me.

When my back was against the wall with thousands of orders, it was *people* who showed up to help me.

And if I didn't have their complete respect, they may never have called into their real jobs just to come to help me even after years of not working with them.

The truly unreal thing about this is that even years later, every time we go back to visit family in Wisconsin and we make a Target run, we will often run into the people who helped us overcome insurmountable odds on that cold December day, and they always ask if I need their help. They are always willing to work for me again.

This may seem like an unimportant smidge of information, but I truly think it's worth noting.

People will always be the catalyst to push you forward.

We live in a world where we don't appreciate the people who helped get us to where we are today. Always remember to take care of the people who help you or work for you.

Did I have any idea that 10 years after managing these people, I might one day need their help? Absolutely not. But I always treat everyone I meet with the utmost respect, no matter if they're the CEO or the doorman. I give everyone the respect they deserve, and it has always come back 100-fold.

CHAPTER FIVE

How to Delay What You Desire Most

Maybe I'm not the sharpest tool in the shed because I couldn't see that every time I set a new goal, I was actually delaying my happiness.

I know this seems to be the mainstay in entrepreneurial circles: Goals, Targets, Weekly Goals, Monthly Goals, blah blah blah.

Don't get me wrong. I think goal-setting is essential for anyone who wants to be "successful."

The problem lies in tying our happiness to them. Always thinking, *I cannot be happy until I achieve this goal.*

The other problem is we are not happy when we achieve them. We simply move on to the next goal and the next, never truly allowing ourselves to be happy in that moment.

We live our lives predicated on some future event, and when that event happens, we move on to the next and the next and the next, and so on.

So what does this mean? Stop setting goals? No, that's not the answer.

Stop trying to achieve great success? No, I think that will leave us more miserable than before.

Shoot for great things. Set goals. Be happy when you achieve them, but don't tie your happiness to them. And, most importantly, celebrate when you hit that goal!

Now, that may seem like an oxymoron. How can I be happy when I achieve a goal but not hold my happiness hostage to achieving that goal? By enjoying the process. By enjoying the journey.

I won't remember my goals ten years from now, but guess what I will remember? How I got there.

After I worked my ass off for a couple more months, we decided to take a month-long vacation out west.

So I said to myself "I'll be happy when I can buy myself a brand new truck and take my family out west to my former home."

This was a big turning point for me. So far in the business, I had never taken a cent out of it. We lived very cheaply with the amount of money we were bringing in, mostly living off of Sara's paychecks while re-investing everything else into the business.

Sara and I test drove every truck on the market, finally narrowing it down to a brand new Ram® Rebel. It was everything I ever wanted, dark grey with all blacked-out trim and big off-road tires. I had the dealer-ship find the exact spec I wanted shipped to them.

Up to this point I had never bought a new vehicle in my life. I drove what most people would call shit boxes. I had a ton of $250 cars/truck—not payments—the whole car was $250. We had one nicer vehicle, a Jeep we bought used 10 years prior right before Sara and I got married that we used to take on a road trip out to California for our wedding.

I went to the dealer to pick up my new truck, and I was scared shitless. I'm not sure why. I think I was in shock and still felt like I didn't deserve it. I overcame my fear, signed the paperwork, and drove home in my dream truck.

We went on a 6,500-mile road trip, visited five National Parks, and I got to show my family Colorado, Utah, Arizona, and where I grew up in California.

After almost a full month of traveling across the Western United States with Sara, Sebastian, and Isaac, I experienced my favorite day from that trip.

We woke up in a small town in Utah. I think it was called Blanding. The previous day had been pretty epic. We had spent that day off-roading in Moab, Utah, and exploring Arches National Park.

We baked ourselves at Arches National Park. Even though it was March, it was 80 degrees and sunny, and our Wisconsin skin hadn't seen the sun since September.

I was particularly tired when we woke up in Blanding because once we got to the hotel late that night, we still had to bathe our two kids, read them stories, and get them off to bed. After that, Sara and I still had to shower and clean up.

By then, it was 11 PM. Bedtime for most people. Not for Sara and me. This had become the time of day when we would go to work.

By around 1 AM, Sara was exhausted and called it quits. I, on the other hand, don't know when to quit, so I was up until 4 AM working.

You see, that work ethic my Dad instilled in me is great, but it also never lets me relax. Like, ever. If there is work to do, I do it.

We all got up at 7 AM, had breakfast, loaded the truck, and off we went.

Sara preparing lunch while the boys play happily with their trucks in the dirt at the Valley of the Gods, Utah.

We went off the beaten path a bit, hitting Moki Dugway (which I highly recommend), Valley of the Gods, and Monument Valley. We ended the day watching the sunset at the Grand Canyon.

I know that all sounds relaxing and shit, but have you ever tried spending a month in a car with two toddlers, then taking them to the edge of a cliff with a many-thousand-feet dropoff and no guard rails— to watch a sunset?

Sara was carrying 3-year-old Isaac in a harness on her back, and 4-year-old Seb wasn't permitted to let go of our hands.

Yeah, I wouldn't exactly call it relaxing.

Honestly though, this trip meant a lot to me and my family and always will. We explored Colorado driving up Pikes Peak, then visited the Garden of the Gods. We moved onto Utah and then Arizona before finally making it to California. We drove from San Diego to damn near the Oregon Border on the Pacific Coast Highway in California, visiting the Redwoods and the Avenue of the Giants before heading back home to Wisconsin.

But let's just say that after we got back from our "vacation," we were ready for another vacation!

I did learn a very valuable lesson that day, leaving the Grand Canyon after the sun went down. If you off-road all day there is a good chance your headlights will be so coated with red sand and dirt that you will have about as much visibility as a blind man.

We left the park after dark, with almost zero light shining out from the headlights. As I squinted, just trying to keep the truck between the lines, I saw a flash of what looked like a giant blob that was higher than my truck.

I swerved, barely missing a giant elk standing in the road. After we were clear from the elk, I stopped to clean my headlights (and my pants). I learned two things: 1) clean your headlights after offroading, and 2) park elk don't care.

Okay, I learned a few valuable lessons on this trip. Another is that sand is a lot harder to drive on than you think.

Years prior, on our way to get married, we had taken our first Jeep out onto the sand, but this was a little different. My brand new truck was my pride and joy. I basically drove this thing off the lot and then across the country.

We were sitting on the beach, enjoying the day, and Sara could tell I wanted to take my truck back into the Oceano Dunes (Pismo Beach), but I was a little scared. This truck was not only brand new but it also had to get us home from California back to Wisconsin.

Sara likes to tease, so when she said, "Don't be a Sally, let's go!" And then the kids echoed, "C'mon, dad, don't be a Sally!" That's all it took. I bought a flag on the beach, dropped my tires to 15 psi, and off we went to explore the sand dunes.

If you have never driven in sand, it's kind of like driving in marshmallow pudding—especially in a big truck that just wants to sink. As soon as you get away from the ocean, the sand becomes extremely soft.

We had a blast, drifting, jumping, racing through the dunes. It was all going well until I hit a bowl with a fence line in my path. I couldn't avoid going down into it. I turned, trying to make my way around. It was much steeper than I thought, and I sensed the truck felt like it was going to roll. I turned downhill to make sure we didn't roll over.

I was presented with a new problem, I had to get out—now. I mashed the pedal to the floor, banged off the skid plate, and made it four feet from getting out the other side.

I now had to back down and try to find another way out. It was probably the adrenaline at the time, but I thought I could turn around at the bottom. I was wrong. I wedged the truck into the side of the dune and buried it to the axles. Trying to get out, the tire came off the rim, and I was stuck.

My truck, buried deep in the sand at Pismo Beach Sand Dunes, California.

We were able to flag down a ranger and call a tow truck.

The boys played in the sand and ate gigantic strawberries we had gotten the night before at the farmers market in San Luis Obispo.

Once the tow truck got there, the driver asked me, "Do you want to help me change the tire and get you out of here?" I paused, but when he mentioned it's $300 an hour for his services, I was like, "Hell, yeah, what do you need me to do?"

He said, "We need to dig out that tire so we can put your spare on."

There I was like a fucking badger digging to China. We changed the tire, which is especially hard in soft sand, as you have to place the jack on a shovel so it won't sink. Seemed legit and totally safe ... ish.

We got the tire changed, and he was able to pull me out. I drove from there back onto the harder sand near the ocean. My pride was hurt, but I have a story and memories that will last a lifetime. Sara still jokes with me every time we are in the sand ... "Watch out for those sand dunes!"

I will be happy when I can buy my dream truck and take my family to California.

Check.

Happy?

Well, this time, yes. I was unequivocally the happiest I had been in as long as I can remember.

But here's the problem: I didn't want to leave California.

You see, growing up, getting tossed from place to place and parent to parent, I never had what most people would call a "home." The closest thing I had was my grandparents' house, but it wasn't ever my own home—it was G&G's house.

Always the oddball, living in a place like Wisconsin never felt right. It's a place where everyone pretty much looks and acts the same. If you're not the "good ol' boy" working a 9 to 5 job like everyone else, people look at you funny.

When I moved to California as a kid, it felt like home. I can't explain it, but it was the first place I ever felt like I belonged. Even though I bounced from place to place and school to school, for an outcast like me, that felt pretty good.

Now, don't get me wrong. It's not like I instantly blended in with the locals. When people hear you're from Wisconsin, they immediately think you grew up on a farm. I never lived on a farm. I lived in the city or in the suburbs most of my life.

While most people in Wisconsin don't move more than 25 miles from where they were born, California is more of a melting pot. People of all races, colors, various backgrounds—people from all over the country and the world move to California.

Almost everyone is an outsider, so to speak, so being surrounded by so many other outsiders made me feel like I belonged. We were all outcasts in a way.

On the other hand, most people in Wisconsin are essentially the same. They are born there, they live in the same place their entire lives, they do the same jobs, and they die.

Someone like me, a free spirit, just always felt like I didn't belong in Wisconsin. You know where I did feel like I belonged? In California. With all the other weirdos.

Long story short, visiting California with my family felt like going home. And, by golly, I was happy as fuck to be home. The problem came when I had to leave. I was not happy about leaving, so I set a new goal: "*I'll be happy when* … I move my family to California."

After leaving California and getting back to our home in Wisconsin, I was initially happy to be able to sleep in my own bed and get the kids back into their normal rhythm. After a month of traveling with 3- and 4-year-old boys, Sara and I could get back to a somewhat normal life (if there is such a thing).

But it didn't take long before I started to get down and depressed again.

I started hating everything about Wisconsin. I hated the people, the weather, everything. Why? Because it wasn't California. I wasn't there, so I hated where I was.

This wasn't too good for my overall mental well-being.

Even with all the feelings of discontent growing inside me, I continued to grow the business.

At least when the weather turned warmer that summer, we had some fun with the kids.

As the weather turned colder in October, it was time to plan another trip south. This time to Texas. Since I had been watching Formula One racing from the time I was a kid—and watched it quite a bit with my own kids—we decided to take another two weeks off and spend a week in Austin to watch the Formula One race at Circuit of the Americas. Then, we'd spend a week in Galveston at the beach, actually relaxing. Imagine that!

Sara, Sebastian, and Isaac hanging out on Pit Exit
at the Circuit of The Americas in Austin, Texas.

I had grown a lot during that time in our lives. Sara and I went from running a million-dollar business on our own to hiring out help to do the tasks we really shouldn't be doing but I had been too stubborn to let go of. Finally, I was able to take my first real vacation. Ever.

Yes, I still worked for a few hours here and there, but it was mostly just managing employees and overseeing things from a distance—quite a difference from our trip to California.

Returning home, though, was a shock. I remember the moment we got back to Wisconsin. When we left, the temperature there had been in the 50s, and it was going to be warm in Texas, so I didn't pack a coat.

We left Texas early in the morning and drove all day and all through the night, arriving in Wisconsin around 5 AM. I got out to pump gas in some lightweight pants and a long-sleeved shirt. At that point, it was 20 degrees, and with a stiff wind, it felt like below zero.

I think my balls could have been musical instruments from all the clanging going on. They were frozen. Can you say shrinkage? I could barely bring myself to touch my gentleman sausage in the bathroom as I thought it might shrivel up and go inside me from my frozen hands.

As you can see, my welcome back to the frozen tundra was less than pleasant.

All in all, we got back from our second trip that year feeling good, even with the weather being cold as fuck. I had grown a lot this year from finally "making it," as most people would say.

I was married to the love of my life. Our two boys were happy and healthy and thriving. I had a new truck and a successful business. We went on vacations totaling a month and a half of the year, and I was about to embark on a trip a month after our trip to Texas.

The plan was for me to attend WarriorCon in Orange County, California, where I had lived as a teen with my mom, a place I longed to return to as an adult.

Things rarely turn out the way we expect them to, though.

CHAPTER SIX

The Road to Warrior, Leaving Me More Lost than Before

I felt like I had my shit somewhat figured out and almost didn't go to WarriorCon, which is a week-long event for men who want more profits in their business, more passion in their marriage, and more purpose in their life.

Sara, being supportive, and knowing more about me than I can see about myself, said I should go.

You see, Warrior had transformed my life twice. First, when I was an overweight, depressed, lost man, and again after my back surgery when I was figuring out my shit.

I felt like I almost owed it to the founder, Garrett J. White of Wake Up Warrior, to go.

My entire life transformation happened as a result of finding that first Sean Whalen Facebook post. From there, I was led to Warrior and Garrett, then Jesse Elder, who led me to guys like Ryan Stewman.

Ryan Stewman led me to Adam Stark, who I worked for as an ISA, or Inside Sales Agent. He was a real estate agent like me, but I couldn't work as a real estate agent because I was recovering from surgery. I helped close appointments for him, and I learned a lot from him.

He led me to other people I learned from, which came full circle when

Jesse Elder led me to Ryan Daniel Moran and to E-commerce, which is how I ultimately changed my life and created a million-dollar business.

I owe my success to a few people who I followed online. I listened to every piece of content they put out, bought their programs, and hired them as mentors.

Going to Warrior felt like a homecoming, although you'll see that certainly wasn't the case when I got there.

The trip started off great! I flew into John Wayne Airport in Orange County, which brought back great memories as I always used to fly out of this airport with my Mom back to Wisconsin for the holidays.

My cousin Nick (who lives in Orange County) picked me up at the airport. We went and grabbed some dinner and caught up, and then he dropped me off at the hotel in Dana Point.

The first day, I woke up to a beautiful view of the ocean. I smiled. California felt like home.

Yep, that's me in a suit and tie, attending Warrior Week.

I wasn't quite sure what to expect at WarriorCon. I mean, I knew it was going to be a bit unorthodox because that's Garrett's way, but I wasn't prepared for what I experienced.

The first day at Warrior was a bit of an eye-opener. I thought I would feel at home with these men. I mean, I had lived the last five years of my life by this system. But I didn't feel at home with them at all. Most of the men were mindless tools.

Their biggest problems were they were dicks or couldn't keep their dicks in their pants and were fucking around on their wives. I felt completely out of place—like I wasn't broken enough to be there.

I am a good husband, I love my wife, I am a good father, and I am a fairly good human being overall. These guys were mostly self-absorbed, stupid pricks. And I don't mean their actions were stupid, I mean they were literally stupid. Mindless drones who would easily follow anyone who told them what to do, without thinking for themselves.

They were the complete opposite of me. My biggest problem was getting out of my own head long enough to realize I have a damn good life. I think I am a pretty damn good father and put my family and wife above all else.

These guys were horrible human beings, not smart enough to even be in their own heads. Their biggest problem was keeping their little heads out of other women, if you know what I mean.

So, it was awkward, to say the least. It was the first time in my life I didn't feel fucked up enough. I realized in that moment that I may not be that bad after all. At least I was a good father and a good husband—the two most important jobs in my life.

I will say this. For as many douchenozzles and idiots that were there, I did meet a few people who were battling the same demons as me and were good men. I also appreciated going because it taught me some things I didn't know about myself. I don't fault Garrett for the people there. All sorts come to events like this, and the event itself was amazing. I had to dive inside myself to finally learn what my biggest problems were.

I may have not had the problems some of these men had, but I did realize quite a few things. I am an emotional mess in the complete opposite way of most people. My biggest problem was letting anyone into my life.

My entire life, I was more of a loner. I never let anyone see the real me because I didn't trust anyone. After having serious issues with both of my parents, and all that I went through with them, I trusted no one.

Sure, I had friends. In fact, most people throughout my life thought I had a lot of friends because I can instantly get along with anyone and make people laugh (comes from years of moving around so much), but I never built any deep bonds.

The only person I fully trusted was my wife Sara. Hell, we dated for four years before getting married. It took many years before I trusted anyone else and this trust became one of the keys to my finding myself, as you will see later on.

I also learned why I had such a hard time after my back surgery, not physically but emotionally. For my entire life, I always had to be the strong one. Even with my Mom, I was the strong one who took care of us.

Throughout my relationship with Sara, I played the part of the strong one. I never allowed myself to show pain or be vulnerable. I kept everything bottled inside.

When I was a kid, I was quite emotional and cried a lot. I had been through a lot with both parents, but my Dad wasn't allowed to show emotion when he was younger. He did what he knew best and yelled at me whenever I cried.

I was not allowed to cry or show emotion in any way, and I was ostracized if I did.

As I grew older, I learned never to cry or show emotion. No vulnerability whatsoever, which means I never let anyone see the real me. I think this is why I got so fucked up in the head. That's a lot of shit to hold inside for so many years, and it can mentally break you.

Imagine trying to recover from surgery without feeling like you can open up and be vulnerable, or trying to get back on your feet financially after having the rug pulled out from under you again and again.

The most valuable thing I got from the WarriorCon trip was finally opening up to a few other men. I also realized a huge flaw in my emotions and what happened after my surgery.

Prior to my surgery, even before I met Sean Whalen and started to shift my life, I always appeared to be the strong one in my marriage. I refused to show weakness. I helped carry the family through being homeless, through all of Isaac's surgeries, through every hard time life threw at us. I was the rock.

But when I had my surgery, something shifted. I was no longer the rock. I was broken. Both mentally and physically. Here I was, 30 years old, and my wife had to wipe my ass because I was fucking crippled.

I was no longer the strong one, and I didn't know how to handle it.

Don't look at this the wrong way. Sara is an absolutely amazing woman. She picked our family up from ruin when I fell apart. She got a better job, worked more shifts to make ends meet, and put food on the table.

She helped take care of me and the kids, pushed me to get up every day and walk even though the doctors weren't quite sure I would ever walk normally again.

She was a fucking rock. Not just a rock—a damn mountain peak.

When I fell down, she stood up and took care of us.

I appreciate everything she did, but that was a problem, too. I had never shown weakness to anyone, ever, and now she had seen me weak. I had no idea how to cope with it. Deep down inside, I held onto some form of uncertainty knowing she had seen me weak. Somehow I felt as though I was now a lesser man.

I think this is why I fell down such a huge mental hole after my back surgery. I lost my place. The only thing I knew. I didn't know how to handle this new feeling.

Don't get me wrong. Our marriage was great. We loved each other fully, and we were still best friends. But after my surgery, I even shut Sara out, unable to handle her seeing me in weakness. I pretty much shut everyone out.

I am not proud of this, and from the outside, no one would know anything was ever going on. But from the day of my back surgery to the day I left for Warrior, I didn't let Sara or anybody in.

The day I left California I went for a walk on the beach trying to take this all in. I walked alone for hours. I mustered up enough courage to send Sara a video to tell her how much I loved her and how I looked forward to restarting our lives in California together.

That night, my flight came in late. I arrived at the airport in Madison at around 11 PM. Sara came to pick me up with the boys, and I have never been so happy to see anyone in my entire life. I ran to Sara when I saw her; I held her close and squeezed her. I love this woman so much.

How did I keep my emotions from her for so long? It felt amazing to see her and hold her—like nothing in this world mattered but her. And in all honesty? That's all that has ever mattered to me. Sara, Sebastian, and Isaac. That's who I was doing all this crazy shit for. The four of us.

To be really honest, I would be nothing without Sara. My soulmate who has always picked me up and championed me through thick and thin. Every time I wanted to quit, she pushed me forward. Every crazy dream I had, she said go for it. She has always been the rock, not me. I just *thought* I was the rock. She is the real hero.

Life was good for the next month. Sara and I finally felt like us again. We would need this strength through the coming year when times got tough again.

CHAPTER SEVEN

The Hardest Day of My Life

You may remember that I mentioned in the first chapter of this book that my younger son Isaac was born with clubfeet. Those feet required a whole series of surgeries, and now we were coming up on a big one.

It was scheduled for January 2. The purpose of the surgery was to cut and then re-attach one of the tendons slightly lower on the outside of each foot. It was meant to pronate (turn out) the foot to its proper position. We were told it would be the final operation of the series Isaac had undergone since birth. This would be the third time he would have to completely re-learn how to walk.

One of the reasons we'd stayed so long in Wisconsin was for Isaac's doctor. He was a recognized expert on clubfeet, and we continued to put our complete trust in him. We wanted the best for our son.

The big day came, and we dropped older brother Sebastian off at school before settling in at the hospital. The operation was scheduled to last four hours, but it lasted seven. I ran out to pick up Seb from school, and then we held our vigil in the waiting room at the hospital.

The doctor finally emerged and told us that the surgery had gone well. A nurse told us that one of us could go be with Isaac as he woke up, and Sara insisted it be me.

Walking into his room was a shock. His eyes were closed. What stopped me in my tracks, though, were the rods sticking out of his toes and running back to his ankles.

Both legs were in casts, and blood was visible all over them.

The nurse saw my reaction and grabbed a chair for me.

I couldn't hold him in my arms, so I sat next to him, holding him as closely as I could.

He slowly started waking up. He smiled when he saw me, and it was one of the most beautiful things I'd ever seen. Soon, Sara and Seb were allowed to join me, and we watched him doze in and out of sleep.

He was moved to a room upstairs, and the three of us followed. That night, Sara took Seb home, and Isaac and I watched the *Lego Batman* movie before he drifted off again.

Around 10 AM, Isaac woke up in intense pain. The meds from surgery had worn off, and now he was uncontrollable. The pain was bad, but so was the fear I saw in his eyes. The little guy didn't know why his world had suddenly descended from euphoria to cruel and fierce pain. Despite my efforts to prevent it, this four-year-old fireball managed to pull out his IV while thrashing in agony.

Inserting another IV was impossible—it was like trying to bathe a cat. So, we tried oral meds, but he threw them up. Which led to the question of how much oral medication actually got into his system. Because that was an unanswerable question, they couldn't give him any more.

That night was the longest of my life. It was a cycle: after a safe amount of time, he was given meds that finally stayed down, and he'd fall asleep. Twenty minutes later, he'd wake up again crying and screaming. Nurses managed to get another IV in him, but he'd rip it out again, even with me trying to restrain him. And on and on it went like that all night long.

Not being able to help your child who's suffering so deeply is the worst experience a parent can have. All I could do was hold him and assure him that I was there. I lay there in that tiny bed, covered in vomit, trying and failing to ease his suffering.

Around 5:30 AM, he was able to keep down some anti-nausea meds. That opened the door for him to take and absorb the full load of oral pain meds. Once that was accomplished, they were able to get another IV in him, and at 7:30 AM, he finally fell fully asleep for the first time.

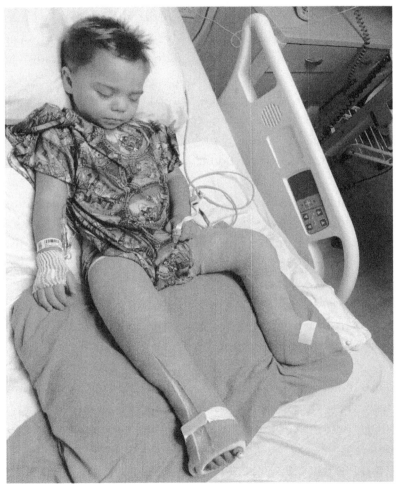

Isaac, finally asleep after an excruciating night after surgery.

At 9 AM, Sara got there, allowing me to crash on the couch in Isaac's room. I'd been up for nearly two days, and, combined with the emotional stress of the night, I went out like a light.

When I woke up a few hours later, I found that Isaac and his medical team had gotten in front of the pain, and he was doing much better! Sara found him a little wheelchair, and the two of them wandered around some. She wanted time with him, so I did the school pickup duty, fetching Sebastian, and I went home to let our dog Luci out.

As Seb and I were returning to the hospital, Sara called to tell me the hospital was going to discharge Isaac. My first response was not a happy one. After the night he (and I) had, I didn't think he was ready.

Sara, who's a nurse at that hospital, wanted to care for him at home, as long as it was a safe choice, but we argued about it. I felt she didn't understand what the previous night had been like. Even if his condition warranted his coming home, it wouldn't be easy caring for him.

I wasn't convinced even as we started home with him. We continued arguing about it. Halfway home, Isaac melted down. We'd thought we were ahead of the pain, but every bump in the road sent flaming misery down his legs and feet.

She did come to understand what Isaac and I had gone through, though. Neither she nor I slept the next three nights as we shepherded our boy through his own private hell.

I took a month off work to help care for him. My business continued, though, and while I had all kinds of time to get in my head and sabotage my happiness journey, I stayed on a pretty even keel. The reason, I think, was that I was determined to keep coming back to being appreciative of everything I had and was.

I had plenty of money in the bank, and I was spending every day with my son. One month off turned into two, and I became deliriously aware of his courage and resilience. We even began to work out together. He built his muscle strength up by pulling himself around. And I began to lift him, at 40 pounds, and his leg casts, at 20 pounds, swinging him like a kettlebell.

Now that Isaac was on the mend and his final surgery was done, our last obstacle to moving from Wisconsin to the West Coast was gone.

That thought was both liberating and scary. Having the answer to my "I'll be happy when ..." right in front of me was scary. Will I really be happy? What if I somehow screw it up?

The question of whether or not I deserved happiness began to reassert itself. This felt like my last possible life goal. I had the wife and family I'd always dreamed of. I had the business I'd wanted. And the freedom.

This was the final one. "I'll be happy when I move my family to California." I'll finally be home, and I'll be happy.

So, while we sold off some stuff and told friends and family we were planning to go, that nasty little whisper in my head—the one suggesting I didn't deserve it and therefore will fuck it up—started and wouldn't shut up. I decided to drown that voice out by doing what I did best: work.

The work this time had a very definite goal: sell the business.

I interviewed several brokers and made my choice. Together, we announced my business was for sale. It generated a lot of interest, and I spent time with potential buyers on the phone, sifting through the prospects. Many of them submitted letters of intent (LOI).

I narrowed them down to one. Everything looked good for him as our buyer, and we drew up the offer, which was a legal, binding offer. Just as we were about to sign the papers, he announced to us a new set of terms he wanted.

Ah, hell no. I told him to take a hike, and he did.

So, we were back to square one, making and fielding calls. We narrowed it down, drew up the contract, and, bam: the same thing happened. The guy changed the terms at the last minute, and I told him to hit the bricks.

I listed my business for sale in June. Our plan was to move at the end of summer, but six months later, we were still there. Waiting. Frustrated as I was, my broker talked me down a few times from just walking away and not selling. So, I continued to focus on this one thing: selling.

This wasn't just a project my broker and I were working on. And he wasn't the only one trying to keep me on an even keel. In fact, Sara did most of that work.

While everything appeared fine with us as a happily married couple, I'd gone back to being completely closed off from her. It was the deeply-conditioned response I had to stress—the way I'd handled things from my earliest days ... the way I assumed everyone was watching me and getting ready for me to fail.

That false-face thing I did, projecting control and strength, bothered her because she knew it wasn't honest. I wasn't honest. And she confronted me with that fact.

We were sitting across from each other one night. The kids were in bed, and the house was quiet. She sensed—she knew—I wasn't doing fine, and she told me so.

I couldn't look away from her.

I had been emotionally distant from Sara. We still loved each other, had sex, went on dates, you know, the usual husband and wife stuff. Inside, though, I was closed off. I showed no pain, no feeling, no emotion.

If she asked how I was doing, I would lie and say good or fine. She knew I wasn't fine. She knows me better than I know me. Things were better after WarriorCon, and I understood why I did these things. Still, I had once again reverted back to my old ways.

I shut down and shut out everyone again.

Something after Isaac's surgeries made me shift back very quickly. Maybe it was the actual surgery and seeing him in so much pain. Or maybe it was having so much downtime to think.

So, there we sat, eye to eye, and for some reason, that hard outer shell cracked. I finally let her in again for the first time since my back surgery. I wasn't fine. I was an emotional, fucking wreck.

We talked and I cried, and I mean I cried a lot. For one of the first times since I was a child, I cried in front of someone else. Sara and I had been together for 12 years at this point, and she had never seen me cry.

Everything came flooding out.

Here are my journal entries from that night and the next night:

Journal Entry #1

I broke down tonight, for the first time in a very long time.

I cried for two hours.

Sara and I talked a lot about why I am unable to let go. Trying to figure out why I can't forgive myself, why I can't let this shit go.

It was a deep conversation. It all goes back to my childhood. How I always feel like I am not enough and how I never truly let anyone into my life.

I had some fucked up programming from childhood. How I never did or do anything for me.

I'm always trying to prove everyone wrong.

How I feel like I didn't deserve my success.

So I kept burning everything to the ground.

There was a reason I couldn't move forward. It was because I held onto everything from the past. How I held onto and had been unable to release the guilt. How I am unable and never learned how to be happy.

Why I almost lost everything because I wasn't doing it for me.

I was doing it to prove everyone was wrong about me.

How I feel like I didn't deserve success and happiness because I was unworthy and was told I would never do anything with my life.

I learned more in those two hours talking to Sara about myself than I did in the previous 33 years of my life.

I learned quite a few things.

My past doesn't define me. I need to let others in. I need to cry and realize I'm only human. I can make mistakes now and again. I can't hold onto this cold façade that is not me.

I was very emotional growing up and was screamed at and criticized for crying. That's not how life is, I hadn't had these emotions or let it out and cried for 20 years. I need to cry. It's ok to let that shit out so I don't self-destruct. I need to let others in.

I learned tonight that I burn everything to the ground for two reasons.

1) I don't feel like I deserve to be successful, and

2) I'm not doing it for me or my family. I'm trying to prove everyone wrong, that I was going to be successful.

I came to the realization that we do deserve success.

I worked my fucking ass off to get here.

This shit wasn't blind luck. I didn't fucking trip, slip, and fall upon success.

I worked for year after year after year working on myself and reading business books and self-development books and things to better my mind.

I failed over and over again, always getting back up on my feet to give it another go.

Everyone else was watching TV, but I was feeding my mind with knowledge. At every break, when I worked a job, I was reading. I was writing and working on myself and my business.

Sara and I deserve everything we have built. We deserve our success because WE created it. Fuck the haters and the doubters, I am doing this for me and my family.

I have nothing to prove and I need no one to prove anything to me. I don't need to prove to anyone I am successful. That shit is for the Joneses.

I am going to do Me. I wrote down Jesse Elder's quote, "Nothing to Hide, Nothing to Prove," many times, but I didn't actually believe it or live it.

I was still hell-bent on proving everyone wrong, but why?

Think about that. Why?

Does it really matter that you proved everyone wrong if YOU still feel empty on the inside?

People, in general, are good people. We get into our own heads to show the world we are better than them or they were wrong about us, but here is the funny truth: No one gives a flying fuck.

We are all so busy living our own lives we don't give two shits about other peoples'. But we still beat ourselves up over nothing.

Fuck that noise.

I am here for me and my family, and that is all that matters.

The same holds true for all the guilt and shame I've held onto for being a failure.

What it boils down to is worrying about what my family and others think.

But all my family cares about is me as a human being and as a father, and at that, I am awesome.

My wife and kids love me and I love them. I'm a great husband and father and my wife supports me in everything I do.

My kids think I'm a great dad and that is all that truly matters. I can let go of the bullshit and guilt and feeling unworthy. My family isn't holding onto it. It is me that is, and that's not helping anyone.

Let go. Breathe. This, too, shall pass.

Journal Entry #2 (the next day)

These past few days since my breakdown have had their ups and downs.

I have been working through a lot of shit and have been continuing to work through it.

I have been letting go, bit by bit, and I feel like I have made some progress.

I am starting to feel like me.

I've been present with my kids, having random dance parties, chasing each other around the house, being the fun, happy Dad. Spending time with my boys.

I had a great Thanksgiving.

We went up to La Crosse to visit Grandma and Grandpa. I think we made Grandma's day; she was so excited to see the boys.

The smile on her face made a smile come to mine.

For years it seems I had lost my fun-loving, big-hearted nature.

I don't know why, but business seemed to turn my heart cold.

It wasn't the business's fault.

The business is great and gave me the freedom to be with my family.

It was my mindset that was horrible.

Thinking I had to be something I'm not just because I had created success and owned a business.

I can be me no matter what.

It's all I can be!

———————

What Sara helped me see, first of all, was that I did deserve success.

A business like the one I built doesn't just fall together.

It requires trying and failing and getting up and trying again. You do this over and over without ever giving up hope. Though every fiber in your body wants to quit, you still keep going.

It requires implementing the knowledge gained by engaging in a lot of labor over a long period of time.

The fact that I built it proves I deserve it.

And if I couldn't believe I deserved it, I absolutely could believe *we* deserved it.

I could trash my own efforts. But hers? No way.

She was right there at my side. Seeing how she had helped me and how her help was instrumental in what we built, I could easily see the cause-and-effect going on.

It helped for me to observe it from a third-person point of view because I seemed to be blinded to logic looking at it from first-person.

Several realizations began to dawn on me concerning my need to prove myself.

Most people in my life aren't watching my every move, remembering my mistakes.

They don't give a flying fuck because they're busy living their own lives.

Most people just aren't paying attention to me!

Maybe they care about me when they're talking to me, but after that, I'm little more than a detail they can catch up on later.

That means that I've spent my entire adulthood beating myself up over nuh-thing.

All that guilt and shame over being a failure is just so much wasted energy going out into the void.

My wife pays attention to me every day, and so do my kids. But, folks, that's about it.

Everyone else is in their own little world, paying close to zero attention to me.

So, they're the extent of my little audience. As long as I'm there for them, paying attention to each of them, that's pretty much all I need to concern myself with.

To everyone else, I'm just a character in the movie of their lives—and an extra at that.

I ring the bell and deliver the package to the stars of that film, and then I'm gone.

If I can be me—just me—to Sara and the boys, and to the people who know me and forgive me and my imperfections, then I'm free.

Pushing against all that ingrained shit was a full-time job, and I was already working full-time at my business and trying to sell it.

We're talking three full-time jobs at once, which is to say that undoing my early programming took every bit of discipline I had.

I was struggling to let go, to believe I was successful, to believe I deserved this life.

I was still trying to sell my company, trying to force it, just so I could get that, "I'll be happy when I sell this company ..." box checked and then move on to, "I'll really be happy after it sells and I can move my family to California."

The problem was I wasn't ready to let go.

If you think selling a company you built through years of blood, sweat, and tears is easy, think again.

The monetary rewards don't mean squat to the emotional connection you have from building it. It's like having a baby and then giving it away or selling it.

I struggled a lot.

The reason the first two buyers fell through is that subconsciously, I wasn't ready to sell. If I sold it, then I would have to admit I was successful. So, each time, deals would fall apart.

I had no other choice but to admit to myself that I deserved this life, and that scared the shit out of me.

Finally, one day ... The Voice, God, The Universe, whatever you want to call it, was like, "Hold my beer and watch this. This motherfucker is finally going to change, and I'll make him change the same way I did it the first time. By crippling him till he wakes up."

CHAPTER EIGHT

Willing to Walk

I woke up. It was a day like any other day. It started with a twinge in my back. I was used to small spurts of back issues, so I thought nothing of it. Maybe I pulled something at the gym.

By the next day, I was unable to walk.

My back completely seized.

Not only was I hunched over forward, but also my back was locked over to one side. My torso was completely twisted and hunched over to my right side. I was unable to straighten up.

The pain was unbearable. I couldn't walk. I could barely move, locked up on the floor in my living room. In tears from the pain.

"What did I do to myself?" I thought.

What did I do to deserve this again? This is the last thing I need. I am in the middle of selling a company so I can finally be happy.

The next two months were two of the most excruciating months of my life. It was a complete repeat of the first time.

My days were consumed with doctors' appointments, physical therapy, back injections, and chiropractors.

I slowly got somewhat better.

At least I wasn't hunched over to one side. I could barely walk now.

And then it hit me.

This is exactly the same as the first time.

What am I not listening to?

What sign did I miss?

What am I supposed to be doing?

Then, a funny thing happened, I listened to that little voice we all have in the back of our heads. The one that is trying to get you to follow your heart and not your brain. I listened to what it told me, and not only did I listen but I also did what it said ...

I let go.

I let go of all the bullshit and stress.

I stopped forcing the sale of my company.

I decided I was ready to let go of my company, but I also decided it was OK whether it sold or not. I would be happy either way.

I stopped forcing the move to California.

I realized I was completely happy where I was.

I still wanted to move to California because I like it better there, but I was happy being in Wisconsin.

And I realized I'd be OK if life took me in an entirely different direction. I'd be happy if I eventually decided to move someplace else.

I let go of it all.

Then, this funny thing happened.

I got better.

The stress and pressure I had been putting on myself year after year was tearing my body and my mind apart.

But then I let go.

There was no longer any more, "I'll be happy when ..."

There was just:

I will be happy here. Or in California. I will be happy if my company sells. And if it doesn't, then I can still be happy.

It was miraculous.

My back got better and so did my mind.

The funny thing is ... when I let go of tying my happiness to the outcome, everything just seemed to flow.

The sale of my company quickly moved forward.

I found the perfect buyer, who is an amazing guy.

My mentor Ryan Daniel Moran reached out to me to ask if he could feature me in his book to tell my story.

I was so inspired by him that I sat down that night and started to write this book.

Not because I had to or because I wanted to be a successful author or make money—just because I could.

Business relationships with people I barely knew started to form.

I knew with utmost certainty things would happen.

I knew beyond a shadow of a doubt that I would sell my company.

The difference was I placed no pressure on it.

I was willing to walk away from the whole thing.

And that's just what I did.

My willingness to walk away emotionally opened up my ability to walk physically.

A shift happened that completely changed the trajectory of my life.

When I found myself willing to walk away from it all, willing to give up the dream of "I will be happy when" ... when I found myself completely happy in the moment ... that's when everything started to change.

As I slowly began to shift my thoughts from, "I'll be happy when I sell my company," to "I am happy now," things started to improve—not only with my body but also with my mind, then with the sale of my company.

As I started to let go, another buyer appeared. Things were a bit different this time. We still had our ups and downs. Everything in the deal was taking way longer than it should. This time, though, I wasn't forcing it. If it sold, it sold. If I kept it, I could still do what I wanted with my life.

It did get to a point that I almost walked away, and the funny thing was, I was ok with this decision. We had done extension after extension on the contracts and everything had dragged on for months and months.

We were four days from the expiration of the purchase contract, and they wanted another extension. I simply said, "NO."

I thought, *I have nothing to lose here. If I keep the company, I am good, and it still makes plenty of money. But if we don't close, everyone else has a shit ton to lose. The buyer who really wants the company doesn't get to buy it, and all the brokers, bankers, and others involved could lose their six-figure commission checks.*

It was utterly amazing how fast everyone got their shit together.

Four days later, we closed. The buyer got the business, and I got a bunch of zeros added to my bank account.

Sitting in our kids' school parking lot on the day of closing, we handed over control and got confirmation of the wire transfer. All we could do was wait. Every 30 seconds, I would check our bank balance to see if the money came through yet.

There Sara and I sat, waiting in the car for the boys to get out of school, and it hit. We both cried and squeezed each other. All those trials and tribulations and we finally had the payoff. I'm sure we both looked a mess when we got out to grab the kids, but it didn't matter to us.

I basically handed over my baby that day—something I had spent years building. It was not easy. It was exhilarating, but it was also one of the most stressful days of my life.

CHAPTER NINE

Create Your Own Pattern Interrupt

During the first phase of my business, I was so damn busy, I never had a chance to stop and get in my own head and fuck everything up.

I had also been using the ol' "I'll be happy when …"

I had said to myself, "I'll be happy when I'm my own boss …"

Check. Still not happy.

"When I have a business where I have freedom …"

Check. Still not happy.

"When I buy my dream truck …"

Check. I bought a brand new truck. (Now, this might not seem like a big deal to you, but this was the first time I had ever bought a new car.)

"When I buy my wife the brand new Jeep Wrangler Rubicon she's always wanted …"

Check. Still not happy.

Nope, still not happy.

I was actually pissed off at myself because I should be happy, right? I mean, I had everything I set out to achieve just a few years ago. I went from fat, bankrupt, and homeless to having everything I had said would make me happy.

But I was still telling myself, "Oh! I know! I'll be happy when … and when … and when …."

How is that possible?

You may think I'm crazy. Hell, I probably am. But if you look deep at yourself, chances are, you do the same thing. Always wanting the next thing.

You may not even use the word "happy," but that's the word I started using when I was seven, and it stuck. I'd think, *All I need is a car. Then, I'll have freedom.* Or, *When I meet the perfect woman, my life will change.*

Happiness has a funny way of disguising itself as other things.

You may not use the word "happiness," or the phrase, "I'll be happy when," but I'm damn sure that if you think you're going to feel differently when you get that dream house or car or job, you're still going to be faced with your own internal demons.

Your external circumstances don't rearrange your internal landscape.

On the outside, I'm sure everything looked amazing.

The problem was my conscious self hadn't had the time to catch up to my subconscious self, and that was a big problem. I may have worked my ass off to get all these things, but because I hadn't figured out my mind, deep down inside, I felt I didn't deserve any of it, which means I tried every possible way to fuck up everything I just created.

You see, your mind can be your greatest asset or your worst enemy. As you can plainly see, I didn't get to where I was out of sheer luck.

I made some very difficult decisions and pushed through obstacle after obstacle to create the success I was experiencing. But my brain didn't see it that way. Not when I looked at myself. I felt unsuccessful, no matter what I accomplished.

I would work my way up, up, up, reaching higher and higher, busting my ass day and night, and when I would get to the point where I should be happy (because I had previously stated "I'll be happy when I get here"), I would delay my happiness with a new "I'll be happy when...."

I would start the loop all over again, just like the beginning of the story. Just like my mom.

I needed to change the programming behind the operating system.

Have you seen the patterns in your own life as you've read about the patterns in mine?

We all do thousands of things every day without ever thinking about them. Let's consider breathing again.

Stop for a moment and focus on your breathing. When you stop focusing, you don't stop breathing. You are breathing all day, all night, till the day you die. You do this without ever even thinking about having to take that breath in or out.

The funny thing is, if you want to, you can disrupt that pattern. You can take huge, deep breaths in on a moment's notice if you decide to take action and disrupt the pattern.

That is a pattern and a way to change it. I do this all the time. I will sit down and meditate by taking deep breaths and focusing on my breathing. This deep breathing is a pattern interrupt of my more stressful breathing. Doing this has had a profound effect not only on my breathing pattern but also on my mind.

Now, this section is not about meditation but about the fact that we all have certain habits and patterns in our life. Those patterns can be broken if we make a deliberate effort to change them.

CHAPTER TEN

Never Enough

All this time, I was telling myself, "California or bust."

We knew what we wanted in the new home we would make together: sunshine, a moderate climate, and the stunning landscapes we, as outdoor lovers, wanted.

We loaded up Sara's Jeep Rubicon, tossed the boys in the back, and hit the road. It was June and the weather was perfect for a top-down Jeep road trip.

We had five specific places we wanted to check out. San Diego and Orange County had always been our target, and they were at the top of our list. We also wanted to check out the Central California coast.

But we decided to check out two places in Utah, too: St. George and Park City. During our earlier wanderings, something in me had resonated when we were there, and I just wanted to see if it still did.

When we got to San Diego, we checked into a wonderful Airbnb for our first week. What made this remarkable was that for the first time in my adult life, it wouldn't be a working vacation. It was to be a *vacation*-vacation, and I didn't know how to do that.

We had fun, of course. We went to the San Diego Zoo and SeaWorld®, places I'd been to as a kid. We went to LEGOLAND®, up in Carlsbad, which was a new visit for me.

Isaac, Sebastian, and I at the entrance to LEGOLAND.

We worked our way up the coast, first to Orange County and then beyond, up to Pismo Beach, a place with untouched dunes where we took our first Jeep together onto the beach and dunes on our way to get married in Southern California.

We visited family as we traveled, renewing relationships. I should have been having the time of my life, revisiting as well as finding new places and experiences.

But I began to realize that my heart was slowly breaking.

It wasn't as I'd remembered.

Had it changed, or had I?

I don't know, but it didn't really matter.

This was not the bright, shining place I'd spent so much of my life yearning to move back to, and it was shattering. Now that I had the resources to move anywhere I wanted, my shining mountaintop no longer existed for me.

My son Isaac wanted to celebrate his birthday in the state we had many great memories as a family in. So, we celebrated our last evening together on Pismo Beach with the Jeep parked next to us in the sand.

Sara, Sebastian, and Isaac celebrating Isaac's birthday
in the sand on Pismo Beach.

Then, we piled into the Jeep and drove across California and through parts of Nevada and Arizona, arriving at the southwest corner of Utah the next morning.

I was hot and tired when we pulled up. For eight hours driving through the night, I'd been thinking about my disappointing response to California, taking those thoughts and turning them over, looking at them, and feeding my black mood.

What was once my glowing mountain top, I realized now was a mirage. Maybe California had changed or maybe, just maybe, I had changed as a person. I don't know how to describe the pain, the pain of working all my entire adult life, wishing and waiting for one thing, to suddenly realize it was not what I wanted at all.

My goal, my vision, my mountaintop had shattered, and I had no idea what to do. My lifelong "I'll be happy when I move to California" was gone.

St. George is adjacent to Red Cliffs National Conservation Area, a huge, protected area of natural beauty. The boys couldn't wait to get into the two water parks that were near the house we'd booked, and Sara was swooning at how magnificent the surroundings were. For me, brooding and resting near the pools was pretty much all I wanted.

The next day, though, after I'd gotten the sleep I'd needed, we visited Sand Hollow State Park, a sprawling area that included dunes and a lake. I began seeing what was mesmerizing to Sara: the red rocks, the dunes, the backdrop of high mountains.

We rented an off-road vehicle, a Can-Am Maverick X3, to explore the area. Three miles from the lake was a place called the Top of the World, at the top of Sand Mountain. We could see mountains and desert in every direction. Another four miles south was the border between Utah and Arizona. And Nevada was twenty miles off to the west. Signal Peak, still capped in snow, was behind and above us.

The desert wind blew as I sat there, Sara beside me. I took it in, all of my senses exploring this magnificent part of a world that felt huge. I looked over at her. I said, "Is this the place?"

She smiled, and her eyes had light in them. "We've still got Park City to look at," she said, but she didn't sound like that was a necessary last step to take.

"This seems . . . right. Right?"

She reached over and put her hand on mine. She said, "Let's not fall into old patterns. Let's not second-guess ourselves."

I nodded. "Yeah," I said. "Let's do this!" Well, actually, I said, "As long as I can buy a Can-Am X3, I'll agree to it." Haha!

We looked at several houses, picked one, and signed the paperwork.

We did head to Park City after leaving St. George. It was a beautiful place, but we knew we had made the right call. We also were tired of the snow and cold, so St. George was a better choice for us.

For the last 10 years, all I did was work, from the time I was broke and had to start over to when I moved to Utah, I still lived in the same 1200 square-foot house.

I had built businesses that generated millions of dollars a year, and I ran them out of this tiny house with my office in the basement. I didn't have the fancy houses or toys or motor home I have now. All I did was work, re-investing everything back into the businesses.

I moved to Utah and now have my dream house that is four times the size of my old house. I have the motorhome and Can-Am X3 and "toys" I always wanted.

When we first moved—I remember it like it was yesterday. We traveled across the country with a friend of ours in my wife's Jeep and a 26-foot Penske® truck. Sara and I split off in Northern Utah in the Jeep to get to our new house and get the keys. Our friend graciously drove the Penske (it's slow as fuck when it's climbing mountains, and there are a lot of mountains in Utah).

We made it to our new house and got the keys. As we waited for our friend to make it the rest of the way in the Penske, we just sat on the living room floor of this gigantic (to us) house.

I sat there with Sara in awe of what we had accomplished. Realizing everything we had to do to get to this point, I found myself filled with appreciation and gratitude. It was then I started crying. This house was a mansion compared to what we came from. I was so proud of myself and Sara for how far we had come.

As you may have noticed, finding a "new normal" doesn't take long. We humans are pretty adaptive. So there I am, in my new house, hanging out in my garage in the middle of the week—in the middle of the day—woodworking.

Coming from an E-commerce background, I tend to shop online. We had really trimmed down our belongings when we moved across the country, so naturally, we had to order some things we needed for the new house.

The UPS driver normally just dropped off the packages and went, but today was a bit different. I could tell he had something on his mind, so I started a conversation. Then it kinda just fell out of his mouth. I could tell afterward he felt kinda odd about it, but it was something he had to know.

"Do you even work? I mean, this is a nice house, and every day you are just hanging out woodworking, doing what you want. Does your wife just make a lot of money so you can do nothing?"

I paused. You could tell it didn't come out the way he wanted and he felt maybe a bit embarrassed.

I laughed a bit (and then told him I was a midget porn star—even funnier if you were there because as you may remember, I'm a tall fellow).

I said, "You realize you just delivered me a product."

"Yes," he said.

"Do you know someone has to sell me that product?"

"Yes."

"OK. That's a business. That's what I do. I sell people products they need, and I make money, and the people who buy them are happy because they get what they need."

He paused for a second, then said, "I never really thought about it that way."

The conversation went on for a while after this, about how I got started, the shit ton of work I actually do, and so on.

He left with a profoundly different idea of what he does and how life can be lived: doing what you want when you want and living the life you want to.

I could see the mental shift that took place in his head, and in all honesty, that's all *you* need. Shift your thoughts to shift your life.

Fast forward a couple of months, and we needed more space. Remember, this house is four times the size of our previous one. More specifically, we needed more garage space. "I wish I had this thing, that thing," etc.

Do you see how fast you can normalize even a huge shift in lifestyle? Even though I had everything I could ever dream of, I wanted more.

Now, this is not necessarily a bad thing. We naturally evolve, and expansion is the name of the game in life. We should all strive to better our lives in one way or another.

The problem was I lost focus on how far I had already come.

I wasn't appreciating what we had done anymore. My focus was only on the future, not on the present. I wasn't just trying to get 1% better each day, I was pre-planning in my head multiple levels of the game of life to come.

I think this is where most people get into trouble with being happy with their current life. We are all so focused on what we want in the future—and what others have that we do not have—that we forget what we do have.

We all have the lottery mentality of wanting everything at once.

We don't want to go through the stages and levels of life. We want to shoot straight to the top.

Do you want to know the secret? We all should want a better version of our lives, but the real enjoyment comes from the journey and the process of getting there—not from reaching the actual destination.

CHAPTER ELEVEN

Look Forward, Measure Backward

"Overnight successes" are usually 10+ years in the making. On the surface, it seems as though it happened all of a sudden, but in reality, it was the result of diligently working for a very long time.

Where you are in your life is exactly where you should be. Your life is simply a culmination of the daily actions and decisions that you make.

You have two options:

1) You can blow this off because you don't want to take responsibility for the life you created and stay exactly where you are, or

2) You can take a deep look at where you are and what events lead up to the life you are living. This may be a bit painful, but it is absolutely necessary.

Now let me step back, as I know a million excuses may be popping up in your head. It took me forever to accept this. It is not something that happens overnight. My excuses were valid to me, just like the ones racing through your head are for you.

Here are some of mine:

- My childhood was a clusterfuck.
- My son was born with severe medical issues that put us hundreds of thousands of dollars in debt.
- I was crippled from my back surgery and couldn't work.

As you can see, some of these seem valid. How could I have changed my childhood? How could I have prevented my son from being born that way? These things weren't my choice.

What made all the difference was accepting everything and taking responsibility for my life. I also reframed how I looked at the events in my own head so I could lose my mentality of being a victim. I played that role for years and, trust me, it is not going to help you get anywhere.

I reframed the story of my childhood from "All these things happened to me, and they were bad" to "All these things happened to me and made me exactly who I am today."

And now? I am prepared for anything.

My son's medical issues weren't my fault, but it was my choice to have kids. Since it was my choice, I am not a victim of him having issues. I had the opportunity to make sure he got the best medical care in the world that he needed, and because he went through all this, I can already see how much mental strength it gave him to tackle things in the future.

Once you understand how you arrived at this point, you will have a much better idea of what shifts you need to make to get to where you want to go.

One of my favorite quotes came to me from Jesse Elder. He would often say, "Look forward, measure backward."

Re-read that a couple of times.

Look forward, measure backward.

Look forward, measure backward.

I was reminded of this today as I went up to my office to grab a notebook. Before we moved to Utah, I just threw all my half-used notebooks in a box.

I grabbed one out today and started flipping to find a fresh page. As I flipped through, I came across a page from 2010.

This page was written long before I was my own boss. It was just a few notes to myself to keep me pointed in the right direction.

These notes are as valid today as they were 10 years ago:

Keep reading, keep learning, and know that all this will pay dividends in the future.

CHAPTER TWELVE

Relearning How to Have Fun

Somehow, through this process of building businesses and trying to achieve my goals, I completely lost touch with myself—with what it means to truly live.

You see, as a friend told me, we humans are meant to work, play, eat, sleep, and repeat (sometimes in a different order). Essentially, we are simple beings with simple needs.

As I got so enthralled with building the life I dreamed of, I completely forgot to play.

I was so laser-focused on going from being broke, crippled, and depressed to building the life and businesses I wanted that I never enjoyed the life I had built along the way.

I think this is part of what created the repetitive cycle of more and more without enjoying the process.

I still made sure to chaperone every field trip with my kids, spend time with my family, and have one-on-one time with Sara, but I forgot about me.

I forgot to take care of myself along the way.

I had no hobbies, I never went out with friends, and I never enjoyed anything I had built. I worked 18+ hour days, 7 days a week.

Even on vacation, I wasn't fully present.

Sure, I did stuff with the family throughout the day, but I was on my phone working, long after everyone was fast asleep. I would stay up until 4 or 5 AM, closing my eyes just long enough to fall asleep before waking up a couple of hours later to start the day.

This was a repetitive cycle of *more and more*. I think a lot of it stems from an early feeling of lack. I never wanted to feel like I had felt before. I remember coming out of surgery thankful to even be able to walk, to be free from pain for the first time in years.

I didn't want to waste this second chance I was given. I remember my life of working for someone else, talking to my kids at dinner via FaceTime because I was always at work away from my family.

The funny thing is the thing I wanted most, more than freedom or money, was time with my family. That's why I started this process of self-improvement and started my businesses and worked all those hours tirelessly to build and create.

I was no longer a prisoner of a job; I was a prisoner of my own ambition and my businesses. No longer was I working 12 hours a day for someone else, I was working 18-20 hours a day for myself. I basically just traded one type of prison for another.

After we sold the company and moved to Utah, I tried to relax and have fun. It honestly was the hardest thing I've ever done. It was work to not work! I've always been a workaholic, either in a job or for myself.

One of my favorite quotes is: "How you do one thing is how you do everything." And I always did 110%.

I slowly came around, remembering what it was like to have fun, to spend quality time with my family, my mind present in the moment, and not on the work that I was going to be doing after they went to bed.

What I did was to start taking care of me. Doing the things I always wanted to do. I started down a new journey of self-discovery.

This newfound discovery led me to a Powersports dealer.

When I was a kid, I used to go to dealerships that sold four-wheelers and other outdoor toys like jet skis and such. I used to spend hours there with my cousin Nick.

My Grandma would drop us off, and like two kids in a candy store, we would get on all the four-wheelers and dream of one day having our own.

We used to pretend to go off-roading together. Funny enough, I had been riding ATVs since a very young age at my grandparents' house. It was the dream of owning my own that would cause us to spend hours sitting on each machine in the Powersports dealer.

So as I went down this road of relearning how to have fun, I went back to my roots. I dove back in time to my childhood and tried to remember what fun was. That's what led me to a Powersports dealership.

There were Can-Ams and RZRs (off-road vehicles) as far as the eye could see. I spent many hours there, sitting in them and driving them to find the one that fit me best, but the difference was I wasn't a kid anymore, and I was taking one of these home.

I ended up buying a Can-Am X3. They didn't have the exact one I wanted in the showroom, but they did have one in the warehouse.

*My Can-Am X3, at the Top of the World
at Sand Hollow State Park with my family.*

You know that feeling you got on Christmas morning as a kid? The one where you would walk down the stairs to that beautiful Christmas tree with the glistening presents?

That's how I felt when they delivered it to my doorstep. When the trailer pulled up, it was like Christmas morning, and I felt like a child.

If you're wondering why this is important, it's because this was the start of me relearning how to have fun: a long process that led me to some of the most important self-discoveries I've had in my life.

My entire adult life, I never bought anything for me just for fun. If it wasn't for my family or for the business, I saw no point in purchasing it, so I never bought anything for myself.

I'd bought nothing that was a pure toy, existing simply for the purpose of having fun. That's what my Can-Am was for me, a pure toy with the sole purpose of putting a smile on my face.

This was a huge step for me, a step towards having fun, a step towards finding that inner child who was happy.

CHAPTER THIRTEEN

Realizing Who I Was Always Meant to Become

If you are like me, you like to see how the story ends. How did my story end? Did we move to Utah and instantly find happiness? Well, if you can see from the lessons included here, it is not so much about an ending.

There is no endpoint, there's simply a journey with lessons along the way.

So let's get you up to speed to where I am currently in this journey of life because I learned some of the most important lessons of my life in the last year after we moved.

Moving to Utah was like a breath of fresh air. There is something about a completely new surrounding that encourages a certain amount of change, including the daily routine that can certainly shake up what you know or what you think you know.

Our arrival to Utah set in motion some big changes, not just physically, as in our environment, but emotionally, as in me having to relearn how to have fun. I still struggle with allowing myself the time to have fun. I need no excuses to go out on my Can-Am or to the beach. But there is always a certain part of me that still feels I need to work all the time. That I should not be enjoying myself. That I should be working at that moment.

My Can-Am, although just a hunk of metal and moving parts, showed me something I never knew I wanted or needed, and that was friendship. As I started riding I met a group of other people that rode, a group of people that I now call family.

A funny thing happened when I started having fun for the sake of having fun. When I met people, I was *me*, not the superficial person I had come to be most of my life. I moved so much I never let anyone into my life. People never saw the real me. I always held something back, something in reserve to not let people see my soul.

Something inside me changed when I finally let go and decided to have fun again. It wasn't an overnight shift where I miraculously was a changed man. It was a slow, incremental process.

As I started to meet and become friends with these new people, I started to shift. I don't know if it was the Can-Am or the people or the feeling that I'd finally found a group of friends who accepted me with no judgments ... *but I changed.* I didn't change to become a superficial person. I just started being the real me.

For the first time, I let people into my life. I know this may sound strange to some people, but if you've read this far, you have probably seen a pattern—a pattern of me never being me, a tendency to never let anyone know me on a deep level.

I experienced a change in myself I never knew I needed. I was open about myself, about who I was. I talked about my past and the problems I've experienced. It was quite liberating. Here I was, a guy who had never really trusted anyone in my life (except Sara), openly discussing things that I never would have told anyone before.

I talked with other men—and women, too—but it was huge for me to open up to other men. I talked about my failures, about my bankruptcy, about starting over and over again and again, trying to figure things out. I finally let others in. I showed emotion and not just the tough-guy façade that I had been accustomed to pretending to be.

Then this funny thing happened. I built real meaningful relationships. I feel like I found me again, and when I started being me, these people let me into their lives.

All these people I have met in the last year have become family. It's not that my blood family is bad; quite the contrary. I love them and accept them for who they are. We are just very different.

I will always appreciate everything my sisters and brother did for me when I was a kid. They made sure I had food and the essentials. I will welcome them into my home when they come to visit. But I think I needed to move away for me to realize we are all just our own people—different in our own ways—and that's OK.

This last year was a year of change. You would think selling a company would have been the highlight, but it was just one stop on a longer journey.

Nothing really changed. I was still the same person after selling the business, and to be honest, I wasn't any happier.

Even after moving to Utah, I was still the same person I was before. I had to change on the inside. I listened to the little voice that said, "let go and be you: go have some fun." Being able to let go, to be me, and finally let others into my life, were some of the most important things I have done, not only in the last year but also in my entire life.

By letting people in, I became me.

That's why I wrote this book. This book is for you. I don't know who is reading it, but I hope we get to meet someday.

I hope this book falls into the hands of someone who now sees it can be done.

I hope you see that you can follow your dreams, that you can break that pattern.

You can become YOU.

I have taken the first step. I have put my life story out into the world, something that is honestly the scariest thing I've ever done. What I learned in the last year is that the most powerful thing I have ever done is help people.

I love helping people. I get the most incredible feeling deep down, seeing someone else improve their life. That is why I am here. That is why this book is in your hands.

It is for you to take the next step, to keep moving forward, to find your happy place.

How can you find your own happy place? Let's take the next few chapters to explore that question together. The whole point of me telling my story is so that you can find and define yours. *I'll Be Happy When* is not about defining *my* happiness, as the author, it's about *you* defining your own happiness so you can turn "I'll be happy when ... " into "I'll be happy *now.*"

CHAPTER FOURTEEN

Enough About Me—
Why Are You Unhappy?

I've got a question for you: Why are you unhappy? No, seriously. Why? What is it about your life you don't like? Is it your job? The amount of money you make? Your spouse? Where you live?

You see, if you can't even hit the nail on the head of why you are unhappy, will you figure out how to define your happiness?

When I was writing these very words on this page, I was in a bit of a funk myself. From the outside looking in, I was happy. People wouldn't know anything different.

I live a good life with everything I could dream of, and yet there were still days I didn't want to get out of bed.

I'm being totally honest because I don't want you to read this book and think, "Oh, he has everything figured out." I don't.

I have learned tools, though, and have learned how to course-correct very quickly—like within a few days. Before, I could stay in funks for weeks or even months, while I just went through the daily motions without getting anything great accomplished.

I think there are many parts to the happiness puzzle, and everyone's puzzle has different pieces. So, it requires a lot of self-discovery and figuring out what works best for you.

The problem is everyone wants a magic pill or a specific key to get what they want. Unfortunately, life doesn't quite work this way. I can give you tools (and great fucking ones at that) to help expedite the process, but it is up to you to solve the puzzle.

I think a lot of that puzzle-solving process begins with what I asked at the beginning of this chapter.

Why are you unhappy?

My unhappiness is like a weather barometer. If I am not full of energy and happiness, then there is something off in my life. So I start searching for answers and clues.

Maybe that's the case with you, as well.

Not being fully happy can be like a notice of a storm brewing somewhere, and there is about to be an unexpected downpour. This is not necessarily a bad thing, because it is an advance notice of something that needs to be changed.

You see, I started writing this book for me, not for you. That may sound selfish, but it was a way of getting all these thoughts and lessons swirling through my head out on paper.

As I started getting to the close of writing this book, I stopped thinking of the "now" and only focused on the future. I started worrying about my story being out in the world, about being judged, about the book not selling well, or not being well-received.

The funny thing is that everyone who has heard my story or has seen me come up from the bottom and start over has told me I am an inspiration.

So, I stopped and took a deep look at what was really going on. What I found was quite interesting. I had started writing this for me, but as I went on, I realized how much good this book could do. How much it could help other people. So I decided to publish it after I finished writing.

Here is where the problem came in: I started trying to look into the future, thinking things like, *This book is going to sell millions of copies and, and, and, etc.* Here I was again, placing my happiness on a pedestal with outside circumstances.

I had learned to stop saying, "I'll be happy when …," but the same feelings and habits started creeping in as before. I was putting so much pressure on making this book a success that I lost touch with why I started writing it in the first place.

I think this is the source of a lot of people's unhappiness.

You don't hate your job—you hate that you don't have your dream job.

You don't need more money—you just wish you had the things you don't have.

You are looking into the future and not at what is right in front of you. Expansion and growth are how we naturally progress. You can have a major upgrade in your life, and within weeks, forget how far you have come, leaving you wanting more and more.

Want me to prove my point? Think of a time in your past that you remember fondly. You know, "the good old days," a time when your kids were younger, or a specific situation that makes you smile when looking back.

Now, take yourself back in time, as if this memory is your current reality …

For real. Close your eyes right now and put yourself back there.

You see, when you do this, truly do this, you will realize that at that moment in time, you were only thinking about the future (your current "now"). Back then, you didn't appreciate what was happening.

You look back and think of the good old days, but in reality, when you were living in the good old days, they didn't seem that great because you were too focused on getting past that stage in your life.

What you don't realize is this is a perpetual cycle—a cycle where you are not enjoying yourself in the moment, and you sure as hell are not enjoying the journey.

You live life always putting off your happiness and enjoyment until a future date. The problem is that the date never comes because the second you get there, you are already focused on what you want next.

As you can see, this is a problem. There will always be another level up in life. Even if you get richer than you ever imagined, there will always be another level up.

So if you are perpetually putting off enjoying life until a moment in the future, you are in for a long, disappointing life. Because the only destination in life that closes this chapter of existence is death.

So how can you shift this cycle?

The answer is easy to describe but hard to do.

What is it?

Massive appreciation for what you already have.

That is probably the hardest thing I have learned to do. I naturally want to achieve and do more, but I have to appreciate what I already have; otherwise, pushing forward and getting things that I want out of life will feel hollow.

I realize you may be thinking, "What the hell in my life do I have to appreciate?" But even in the worst possible scenarios, gratitude is possible. For example:

"I got my leg blown off" . . . Appreciate you still have the other one.

"I'm broke as a joke" . . . Appreciate that you have an amazing family.

"I hate my family" . . . Appreciate that you have amazing friends.

Even when I was crippled and unable to work, I still had appreciation. I appreciated my wife for being there for our family.

I appreciated my circumstances because even when I was crippled and unemployable, I was able to stay home with my two young children and spend every day with them. I was able to spend every day while they were young, teaching them the lessons I had learned.

I don't think Sebastian or Isaac would be the same young men they are today if I hadn't spent that year at home with them when I was crippled. By being home, even though I was dealing with my own personal hell, I was imparting all the knowledge I had learned onto my sons, and I didn't even know I was doing it.

Try this. I do it every single night before I go to bed. Even if I've had what could be called a shit show of a day, I do it.

Before I fall asleep, I count out 10 things I appreciate.

They can be as simple as, "I appreciate I was able to have dinner with my family," or, "I appreciate being able to be home to read my son a bedtime story."

It doesn't matter what these things are. It just matters that you start appreciating what you currently have.

If you can't appreciate what you have currently, no matter what you are striving to achieve, you will not be happy when you get there.

So how does this apply to how I said I was unhappy as I started finishing up this book? You see, I was no longer enjoying the process of writing. I looked at the signs and realized I was already pre-planning what the after-effects of writing this book would be.

So, I actively shifted my thoughts from how many copies would be sold, how it would be received, and what people would think, to how I appreciate having the ability to write my thoughts on paper and, if this book finds its way into people's hands, whomever it helps, I will be forever grateful.

See the difference? Writing for a specific outcome versus enjoying the process of writing (and not putting pressure on how this book will be received).

I was re-energized to continue writing, not for the sake of a destination, but for *me*. I feel better, and I know there will be people who will be helped by me putting this out there.

I have no agenda. I am not placing my happiness in jeopardy by putting so much pressure on making this a bestseller.

I appreciate how far I have come in writing, and I appreciate the people this book will help. And if it becomes a bestseller, that is awesome. Because the more people this book reaches, the more people may learn to focus on their happiness.

These lessons are things I have learned through my personal struggles. Please read all of them, even if you think they might not apply to you. You may be surprised how much each lesson will help you out in your own life.

CHAPTER FIFTEEN

Does It Hurt Them or Me?

This is probably one of the biggest lessons I've learned over the years. So, perk up buttercup because it may even be the most important lesson in the book.

If I were to look at 10 people, 9 of them would have this issue. Maybe all 10, in some cases. This was one of the biggest epiphany moments of my life.

It is a key to your personal happiness and may be the one thing holding you back from actually enjoying your life: *letting go of things or people and forgiving them for whatever they did.*

I know what you're thinking. "No shit, Sherlock. Easier said than done." I know. And that is why this is so important for you to get this right.

If you look back at my life and my story, I'm sure you can see similar things that have happened to you. Maybe you had a difficult upbringing or people hurt you over and over again.

I get it. You're angry, pissed off, and letting go is one of the last things you can imagine yourself doing. *"I can't forgive someone for what they did to me ..."*

I understand. Trust me. I was an angry, pissed off person for most of my life.

I didn't have the best upbringing.

I had people close to me screw me over and take advantage of me.

It hurts.

Just reading this, I'm sure there are a few people that popped into your mind.

Did you feel that? Did you feel yourself getting angry or hurt or upset?

Now let me ask you this question.

When those emotions came running through you, who was that hurting?

Those emotions affect you, not them.

I guarantee the person you're upset with doesn't give two shits. They may not even think they did anything wrong. Therein lies the problem. You're angry at people, at things, at circumstances ... and the other parties? They're oblivious.

So who is getting hurt here?

Being angry is hurting *you*, not them.

Does that make sense?

Take a deep look at yourself.

Does holding onto anger or resentment hurt you or them?

Now, you may be thinking, "But my parents were assholes," or "My ex-husband is a dick—and not a big one at that" (haha), or "How could I possibly forgive them for doing what they did?"

That's the thing. It's not about them. It's about YOU.

I know it's hard to see it that way at first. You think you are letting them win if you let that shit go, but that couldn't be further from the truth.

You're playing a game with no winners if you stay angry and resentful. The only one that loses is you because it is affecting your emotions, not theirs.

I'll give you an example from my own life. I'll also show you a way to understand why people are the way they are, which may help you let go of that animosity towards them.

You've probably already figured out that my dad and I never had the best relationship. My siblings and I were bounced back and forth between my mom's and dad's houses. Remember that when I was about 11 years old, I ended up moving to California with my mom, and my dad stayed in Wisconsin with my three older siblings. (My two older sisters were already out of the house, and my brother only had a couple of years left of high school, so he stayed in Wisconsin.) I rarely spoke with him, and I pretty much had almost no contact with my dad for 10 years.

I moved back to Wisconsin and tried to re-build that relationship because I figured one thing out. You are exactly like your parents unless you decide to change it. You see, my dad wasn't a bad man. When my dad became an adult and had kids of his own, he did exactly what he knew. He worked and worked and was never around.

You see, once I realized my dad was who he was because he was doing the only thing he knew, my perception of him and attitude toward him changed. He modeled his own father and did exactly what he had been taught his entire life.

He wasn't purposely doing the things he did, it was just all he knew. So I let go of any animosity. I realized that he had no clue he did anything wrong—this is usually the case—because it was all he knew.

So when I looked at it from afar, he was doing exactly what he knew. He had no idea it was wrong. The only person who was really hurt was me. And that was because I was allowing it to hurt me.

I decided to start fresh, understanding that only I can change that feeling or emotion, not the other way around.

You will never truly be happy until you can get rid of, or fully let go of, the baggage that holds your emotions hostage.

Now, I'm not saying you should just become buddy-buddy with every person that's hurt you before. Some people need to get cut out of your life—make that a lot of people, in most cases.

It is essential that you surround yourself with true friends and family who support you. What I am saying is that even if you cut someone out of your life, you need to come to peace with who they are and not hold onto any anger. Remember it's about you, not them.

I've cut out a huge portion of the people that used to be in my life, but I have no anger or resentment towards them. They are who they are, and I am who I am. I accept who they are, but I also realize in order for me to move forward with my life and be the true version of myself, I can no longer surround myself with people who do not support me.

Worse, I can't be around people who resent me for things I have accomplished in my life.

If you surround yourself with people who champion your successes, life becomes a whole lot easier.

I realized from watching my dad that people do what they know, and if they never take the time to change themselves—to be their own person and not just a replica of what they learned growing up—then you have to realize that is their life and story and only they can change that.

But what if you can't cut someone out of your life? Here's an example that may help.

The reason I've included this is because I know a lot of you will have problems forgiving and letting go for fear of feeling like the other person will "win."

A long time ago, I had two friends who didn't particularly get along. I know it may seem like an easy thing to just cut one person out, but there was a problem: they were both married and their spouses were best friends with each other.

As you can imagine, this caused problems in their relationship because when you hate the person your spouse hangs out with (and think that person's an asshole), things can get tense.

I was always stuck in the middle, friends with all four of them. I hate seeing people unhappy especially when it was a complex situation like this.

Let's call the two friends who didn't get along Jake and Kate. Jake was a bit of a narcissistic asshole at times, but he was also a good person. Kate was great as well, but she let her emotions get hold of her, so they would get into it.

Jake would specifically do things to get a rise out of Kate. Since Kate was emotional, she would get visibly upset, which would make Jake feel like he won.

I talked with Kate about what I had observed. I suggested that she try not to let Jake get under her skin.

It was hard at first because Kate was determined not to let Jake feel like he won by just stopping all the nonsense and letting it go.

Here is the funny thing, though.

Once Kate stopped letting her emotions control her and stopped letting Jake get to her, Jake stopped. He completely stopped trying to get a rise out of her once he realized it no longer worked. He was doing it for the reaction, but once the reactions stopped, it wasn't fun for him anymore, so he quit.

Now, I'm not saying they're best friends (I honestly don't know for sure, since I haven't talked to either of them in years), but when they did have to be around each other, they were no longer like oil and water just pushing each other apart, trying to get a reaction from the other.

I know people have hurt you, and shit hasn't always gone to plan. It's part of life. You can't change what has happened, but you *can* change how you react to it.

Right now you can decide to let go of the bullshit, for YOU. Remember this is about you—not them. It's not about the things that have happened in the past. It's about right now and the choices you can make to move on.

Whenever you feel yourself getting sad or angry or hurt, ask yourself, "Is this hurting them or is it hurting me?" If it's hurting you, then only *you* can make that change, not the other person.

CHAPTER SIXTEEN

Be Afraid and Do It Anyway

One of my greatest assets has been being comfortable being uncomfortable. I know this may seem like an odd concept, but it is quite simple. If it scares me, I will usually do it. I feel like this is the opposite of what most people do. It has not always been this way, but it is one of the key things that has helped me progress in my life.

I am an introvert by nature. I prefer to work from home and just be with myself or friends/family. Oddly enough, in social scenarios, I am also the life of the party and will walk up and talk to anyone and make friends easily. I think moving around so much as a kid and going to so many different schools helped with this.

One of the few things that scares the shit out of me is public speaking (not to mention doing things like I am with this book—putting myself, my name, and my story into the world.)

A good example of my *jump in and do exactly what scares me* principle is me being an ordained minister.

A friend jokingly asked me, "Hey, would you marry me?" (Not as in becoming her husband, haha.) She wanted me to conduct the ceremony for her and her fiancé.

Without a second thought, I said yes. She was like, "Really??" And of course, I said yes. Although I did tell her I was going to wear a banana hammock at the ceremony.

I figured out the details. It cost $67 to order a kit online to become ordained, and we were off to the races—or should I say wedding.

She doesn't even know this as I am always calm on the outside, but I was scared shitless. Not only did I have to stand in front of a group of people, most of whom I didn't know, but it was also her wedding, so it was something I didn't want to fuck up. More than anything, I wanted to make it very special for her.

Even though the whole idea of it scared me shitless, I went all in. We designed the ceremony and vows, and it turned out to be an awesome wedding and an incredible growth opportunity for me.

Why was it such a big deal? Prior to this event I had done almost no public speaking and was scared to stand in front of groups of people. I had now stood up in front of an entire room of people I didn't know, delivered a sermon, and married two amazing people.

Did it instantly make me a pro speaker on stage? Of course not. But what it did do is break that mental block that said, "You've never done that before, so why do you think you would be able to stand in front of a group of people and deliver?"

Now, every time I get on a stage, I can mentally say, *I have done this before*, and go out and crush it.

So many people get held up with thinking, "I've never done that before," or "How do I even do that?" They will use these excuses to put off moving to that next step or doing something they know deep down inside that they should do.

By making it second nature to just jump in and do that thing, even if you have no idea what you are doing, you are now ahead of 95% of people in this world, because you tried it.

You now have some experience in it. Honestly, the "how" is the easy part. The hardest part is mentally just letting yourself do it.

If you're thinking, "How the hell is the 'how' the easy part?" then let me fill you in on a little secret.

There are plenty of coaches and teachers—hell, even Google and YouTube will show you "how."

The hard part is the mental framework behind it that will let you take that first step so you can get to the "how."

Let me repeat that: *How* you do something is the *easy* part.

By running towards things that scare you, you instantly change how your brain is wired.

When a new situation comes up, your thoughts go from:

I've never done that before …

I don't even know how …

I have no experience in that …

To:

How do I do that?

And like I said, if you can get past all the voices to get to the "how" and just move forward with doing that thing and not get stuck in your head, you're golden. You then focus on the mechanics of the situation and problem-solving and just doing it.

If you can get to this phase, you are good to go, because you will instantly move forward and start doing, instead of thinking about doing, and that's a huge difference.

Now I want to add one caveat to this because I think it is very important. Just because I say run towards things that scare you doesn't mean to go charge a semi on the freeway (although removing the warning labels off everything and letting society sort itself out does sound appealing—haha).

You will say yes to things or jump into things head-first, and things won't go as planned. You will fail and fuck up, and things will still go haywire. This is not a freebie to jump into everything and half-ass it.

If you run at things that scare you, you must have a plan. Don't charge at a Mack® truck thinking you're Superman. Physics, knowledge, and preparation still play a huge role.

The whole point of doing these things that make you uncomfortable is reprogramming how your brain works when going into new situations.

For instance, when I agreed to get ordained and host a wedding and marry my friends, I didn't half-ass it and jump onstage drunk and screw up someone's wedding day just to say, "OK, I've done it. I can now speak on stage."

I said "Yes," and I went straight to work. I didn't leave any space for my mind to throw me off track or second guess the decision. I read my minister's book front to back. I met with them. We designed the ceremony and wedding. I made sure to have the legal needs for the wedding worked out.

Once we wrote the ceremony, I read it over and over and over. Several times a day, I would read the entire script of the ceremony so that I could memorize it and have it internalized.

I got a nice binder and printed out the script to have in front of me during the ceremony just in case. I looked at every variable and planned for every possible failure as much as possible to make sure that it went well, no matter what.

Does this mean I'm instantly comfortable being uncomfortable? No. Far from it. I still get nervous and scared like everyone else. The difference is I still do it. I have learned to move from thinking to doing very quickly.

Action is key here. I have found that I get nervous in the time leading up to the event, but once it's go-time, I'm fine, and I go straight to work. This may be different for everyone.

A good example of this is the difference between my wife and myself when we decided to move our family across the country from Wisconsin to Utah. Although I had moved around a lot in my life, this would be the first cross-country move since we had our boys, who were at the time 6 and 7 years old.

In the time leading up to the move (finding a place, planning a moving truck, etc.), I was a bit of a nervous wreck. Once it was time to go, though, I was great. I just went to work packing, moving, unpacking, etc. My wife Sara, on the other hand, was the complete opposite. She was fine in the planning stage and didn't have a care in the world, but once it came time to pack and move, she was a wreck.

It comes down to learning to take action and learning how you deal with these situations. I know I get stuck in my own head. I have to mentally make a decision and immediately move to action; otherwise, I will second guess, doubt it, and my mind will try to rationalize everything.

If I get to the stage of rationalizing it before action, it's all downhill. My mind will come up with thousands of reasons NOT to do something, even if deep down I know I should.

If you take one thing away from this, it should be this: Action is key.

Don't be afraid of change, as change is the only constant thing in this world. If someone were to tell you 500 years ago that you were spinning on a giant rock at 1,000 MPH, you would have told them they were nuts. We now know those are facts, just like you will now know that you are capable of anything you let yourself do. That's the hard part: You have to let yourself do it.

Get out of your head and do something today you normally wouldn't do and see where that takes you. You may be surprised at the results, and that is the first step in reprogramming your mind.

CHAPTER SEVENTEEN

Take Care of You First

What do I mean by "take care of you first"? You know when you get on an airplane and they give you the safety briefing? What is one of the first things they tell you? If the plane should lose air pressure and the masks drop out of the ceiling, put your mask on first before trying to help others.

Do you know why they tell you this? Because if you can't breathe and survive, how are you going to help anyone else out? If you can't breathe, you'll die, and then you can't help anyone else.

Life is the same way. If you aren't able to breathe—i.e., take care of yourself—how are you going to help anyone else out?

This was one of the hardest things for me to learn. For most of my life, I put everyone else first. I felt like it was selfish to take care of me. The reality was I was trying so hard to help everyone else out, I was left burnt out, tired, and in need of help myself.

As I was struggling to breathe (take care of me), I saw that what I was doing wasn't that effective. People follow actions, not words. You ever wonder why kids whose parents smoke end up smoking, even though they were told a million times by their smoking parents not to? It's because we follow actions, not words.

It's the same reason that, no matter how much I tried to help, it only half worked because I was talking the talk but not walking the walk. I wasn't doing what I was saying, so it never worked.

This is a prime example of needing to walk the walk first. You need to take care of you! You need to look at your wants and needs and figure out how to take care of yourself. Now, you may be thinking, "I have a wife and kids, and I need to make sure they get what they need first." Bullshit!

Listen, I'm happily married, and I have two amazing kids. I get it. It's a hard but simple concept. Most of us put everyone else's wants and needs first and are left feeling unfulfilled and burnt out. This doesn't matter if you're a man or a woman or whatever you identify yourself being—it's universal. We are all so busy trying to make sure everything is good for everyone else that we put ourselves on the back burner.

Why is this so important? Because if we want to be the best version of ourselves, we need to take care of ourselves first. Does your wife want to see you unhappy? Do your kids want to see you fat and unhealthy? No.

I guarantee if you truly ask your family what they want, they want you to be happy and healthy above all else.

This all starts with you. It always has. What does that look like in the real world? That's different for every person. For me, that means taking care of my mind and body first. I get up and exercise. I take time to write and read and reflect and make sure my mind is right.

This doesn't mean forget your whole family. Quite the contrary, you are doing this for you, and by doing this for you, you become a better husband or wife, and a better parent to your kids.

You see, taking care of you puts you in a better place to take care of the others you love. By putting on your air mask first, you are saving yourself, and in doing so you are able to save everyone around you.

Just like putting on that air mask, it only takes a few minutes. Take a step back and figure out what you need first. Maybe you need to take a few minutes so you can work out each day so you are healthy and have more energy.

Maybe you need five minutes to yourself to write. Just take some time for you. It will take some practice and learning how to say no. No to people, no to events, no to things that drain your energy and the life right out of you.

By learning how to take care of you first, I can guarantee you one thing. The opposite of what you think is going to happen will happen.

You might think you won't be as good of a spouse or parent, but by stepping back and taking five minutes for you, you will become a more present parent, and your relationship with your spouse will skyrocket. Because guess what? When you are truly happy, it is contagious (kinda like an STD, but in a good way ... and it won't burn when you pee).

You may think this idea is selfish, but it will help others more than you ever imagine.

CHAPTER EIGHTEEN

Design Your Own Life

When I set out to change my life, I knew I needed an exact portrait of what the life I was going to build would look like.

Most people have no idea what they want, and that is the problem. Sure, if you ask someone, they will tell you they want more money or to be healthier, but there is never a real picture of what that looks like— just a vague answer.

I knew if there was any chance of me changing my life, I needed to have a clear picture of where I was going so I could reverse-engineer it to quantifiable goals. This means an exact blueprint of what I wanted (not just, "I want more money").

There I was, crippled, just out of back surgery, broke as a joke, and just trying to feed my family, and I was writing out exactly where I am now.

I still have the journal.

It's funny looking back at it because I was incredibly precise as to what I wanted. Keep in mind that at the time of writing this journal, I was broke, unemployed, and unemployable, and had a severely injured body and mind from damn near losing my ability to walk. I had no idea exactly how I was going to get from where I was to where I wanted to go. I just needed to know what I wanted, and I would work backward from there.

I won't put everything from my journal here, but here are a few of the bullet points:

- I will work from home and be location independent.

- I will chaperone every field trip and school function with my kids.

- I will move to California.

- I will have businesses that make 7-figures per year with a take-home of at least $200,000 per year.

These are just a few of my goals, but as you can see, they paint a pretty clear picture of my future life. I really only had one option at this point and that was to start my own business, or 90% of the items on my list wouldn't have been possible.

From this point on, everything went through this filter before even being looked at as a future prospect. I was dead set on making the life I wanted. I almost lost my life and the ability to even play with my kids ever again. I was damn sure that the life I was going to live was going to be one I wanted.

As I went through the options, nearly every job/business/opportunity got ruled out almost immediately. They all didn't fit with my design, so I didn't waste any time on them.

Then, as I mentioned earlier, I came across Ryan Daniel Moran's video about how to make a million dollars in a year. I was intrigued, so I watched it. He taught Amazon and e-commerce. I started doing a bit more research, and then I put it through my filter.

To my surprise, every single item on my list for my dream life was met (at least on the income and lifestyle/work side).

I went all in, and I mean all in. Some people will come up with excuses for why this can't be done. (No money, No time, No experience, etc.) Sure, I had every excuse at my disposal—I was broke, crippled, and had zero knowledge of e-commerce or Amazon. But when I say all in, it means none of those excuses matter. If YOU have a will, you WILL find a way.

First Problem: I have no money.

I had no money. This is not an excuse. What this means is that I needed to be creative and find a different solution. My solution was going to every clearance aisle, thrift store, and rummage sale. I would buy things I could flip (resell) on Amazon. I did this for 2-3 months. I would buy $20 (all I had) worth of items, list them on Amazon, and once they sold, take that money and buy more items, turning $20 into $40, then $40 into $80, and so on ... until I had enough money to make my first wholesale order ($1,000).

Problem Two: I had no tech skills.

I had no e-commerce/Amazon knowledge. Shit, I wasn't even a tech-savvy person. I have two simple words for you: Google and YouTube. Do you think I had any idea how to flip items on Amazon, or even create an Amazon account? No. Shit, I didn't even know it was a thing. All I knew was I needed money, so I became a knowledge sponge, soaking up new information and learning as I went.

As you can see, the early days weren't all sunshine and roses like all the gurus lead you to believe. It was a lot of fucking work. A lot of learning on the fly and doing whatever it took. Failing repeatedly, until I figured it out.

Life has a way of rewarding those who keep going. Despite all odds, they just keep moving, sometimes backward, but at least they keep moving.

The funny thing about success is people think it's those who make the least mistakes who are successful. Contrary to popular belief, success comes to those who fail, over and over, but keep going, learning from their mistakes and adjusting, until they get it right.

As you can see, being the designer of your life doesn't mean you will go from point A to point B in a straight line. That fucker will probably be a zig-zag that looks like every letter stacked on top of each other with some ancient hieroglyph writing thrown in for good measure.

But you know what you want, where you are headed, and what you are willing to do to get there.

It may take a different path than what you originally thought, but you will end up where you want to be if you stick with it.

The biggest takeaway is that you just need a direction for your life. This direction will help guide you when you are unsure of what path to take. Your point B may even change over time, but if you have a direction, you can skip B and head straight to C, which may be an even better option.

My endpoint was originally California, but that changed, although it was excruciating at the time to admit that I no longer wanted it. I sailed right past point B to point C, which was Utah, and I am so happy that I ended up here.

CHAPTER NINETEEN

Learn to Embrace Boredom

One of the hardest things I've had to do is do nothing. I think we live in a culture of hustle and grind, hustle and grind … I've been doing this since before it was the newest slang from every guru who posts a lot about "hustle and grind" but knows nothing of real work.

From a young age, I have had to work, and I'm not saying that is a bad thing. I have an amazing work ethic that was instilled in me at a very young age, and it has served a purpose in my life. The problem occurs when you get stuck in the hustle and grind phase.

I think life is a series of levels. You can't advance to the next level until you pass this one. Once you lay your smackdown (sometimes it takes many, many tries, just like life), you are then free to move onto a new level and work your way through, until you get to the baddie at the end of the next level, and so on.

There are different stages (levels), and each one has to be completed before you can move on to the next.

What got you to this point in your life won't always get you to the next stage of your life. You see, I hustled for so long and made my way to a certain level, but then I got stuck.

I had now gotten past the hustle stage where I had money and freedom, but now that I had money and freedom, I had no idea what I should be doing. I felt like I still had to be working all the time. If I wasn't working, I had no idea what to do.

At this point, I had two options:

1) Go back into hustle mode, spinning my wheels doing the same things I had known how to do, but not moving on to the next level and expanding. Also, stay unhappy and not enjoy my life, as all I knew how to do was work.

2) Pause, no matter how hard or painful. Take a step back and change what I do on a daily basis. Flex my creativity muscles. Figure out where I want to go with my life and what makes me happy.

As you can see from reading this book, I chose option two. I stepped back from the work to look at the bigger picture. I was a miserable man who knew nothing other than working. I never enjoyed the fruits of my labor. I just kept striving for the next shiny object.

In stepping back and taking some time to inspect my life, I realized the reason I had worked so hard was to give myself this life I currently have, but I wasn't enjoying what I had built. So why did I go through all of this stress, hardship, and building to not even appreciate and enjoy it? It made no sense. I had set out to create this life, which I did. But I was so busy doing the same things over and over that I completely missed that I had created the life I strove so hard to make.

Only when I allowed myself to stop grinding and change from a hustler to a creativity master did things slowly start to change for me.

This book would have never existed if I had not taken the step back to do what was needed to allow myself the time and space to write. Where it gets interesting is how this whole thing affected my happiness.

When I was so busy grinding, I never knew I was unhappy. It was only once I took that step back that I realized I was a miserable fuck who would get depressed if I didn't stay busy 24/7.

You may think, "Duh, then stay busy, and you will be happy." While that sounds simple enough, what is the point of life if all you do is work?

I have a family and two young boys, and the whole reason I got into this world of entrepreneurship was to be present in their lives. Now I was in their lives, but I wasn't present. Even when I was with them, my mind was on work or business, so I kinda missed the goal of this whole self-employed thing in the first place.

So I had to learn how to do nothing—and by nothing, I don't mean mindlessly scrolling social media or watching YouTube. I mean being OK with sitting down and being with my thoughts with no distractions. Giving myself and my brain a chance to flex its creative muscles. Giving myself the space to write this book.

I will be honest; it has been hard. Even sitting here at this moment, I feel like I should be working doing something else. In reality, sitting here writing is making me grow into a whole new person with a newfound idea of what happiness even is, because I am not dependent on an outside event for my happiness. I am OK just sitting here being ME!

CHAPTER TWENTY

Life Is Like a Video Game

What do I mean by life is like a video game? Do you remember playing Super Mario Brothers or something similar?

You would start the game with nothing, not much skill, at an easy level. As you worked your way through the world you would get better and at the end of every level, there was a bad guy you had to defeat.

Do you remember going into Bowser's castle and getting your ass beat senseless? Of course you do, but what happened next is most important. Once you get your ass handed to you and your character reset, you would go right back up to Bowser's front door and have another go.

Sometimes it went well, other times not so much. You would fail and try again and again until you finally had enough skill, knew the tricks, and knew exactly where to stand so that you could defeat Bowser.

Why did you do this, though? Why did you purposely keep failing until you finally got it right and were able to move on? Because you knew you needed to defeat him to move on to that next level. To move onto that new world, you were willing to fail over and over, until you got it right and were ready to level up.

I think this is a great metaphor for life. No matter where you are, there are levels, and in order to get to the next level, it is going to require you to push your limits and fail and keep pushing, until you beat that baddie at the end and level up.

I think a lot of people's unhappiness stems from feeling like they are not where they should be in life and comparing their life to others.

But listen: Right now you are exactly where you should be.

Let me say that again.

Right now, right here, you are exactly where you should be.

Your life is a culmination of every single decision you have made up to this point. If you're not where you think you should be, it is because you should have made different decisions.

I know that's a hard pill to swallow, but it is essential for you to understand. I know you have a lot of thoughts running through your head right now about how that's not true, or if this or that didn't happen, your life would have turned out differently.

You're both right and wrong. Yes, your life may have taken a different path if that hadn't happened. But what if, because that thing has happened, it put you on a better course with more knowledge and better tools to beat the bad guy at the end of the level you are currently on? Bet you didn't think of it that way.

Since I know some of you still have swirling thoughts in your head about how this bad thing has happened and you see no positive outcome at this moment from it, let me give you an example.

When I was crippled, with no feeling in my legs, and rushed off to emergency surgery, there was not a single moment where I thought, "Hell yeah, this is great! This is exactly what I needed."

I couldn't see it at the moment; no one can. But that "bad" situation threw my entire life into a tailspin. Now, I'm not going to say it was hunky-dory. It sucked. I was in a walker for four months and used a cane for another six. I was emotionally, mentally, and financially fuck-ed. We could barely put food on the table.

But … and it's BIG but (like a J-Lo butt—haha), it gave me exactly what I needed at that time. I needed a reset. I needed for my world to be turned upside down.

The situation was not good, but it gave me a reframe on life. Since I no longer could work, I had to figure out a way to make money, which led me to start flipping things online, then to e-commerce, then to building a big business, and then selling that business, which has allowed me to step back and write this book, which could change the course of your life.

You see, I met Bowser in that hospital bed. He kicked my ass. I tried again and again and again to defeat him. Until finally, I had built up enough skills to pile-drive his ass and move on to the next level.

The problem is most people never get to the next level. They give up because they think the world is unfair, and they fail.

What if every time you got beat down, you just got back up, used what you learned, and went on to defeat the bad guy and level up?

What if instead of crying, "poor me," you started taking lessons from everything that has happened to you, knowing this knowledge will serve you in the future?

What if you started saying, "I am exactly where I should be, right here, right now," instead of placing blame on events or people?

What if you started making different decisions that would give you a different life?

What if you re-framed your thoughts and played life like a video game?

CHAPTER TWENTY-ONE

Why New Year's Resolutions Don't Work

If you're like most people, I'm sure you've made a New Year's resolution before. I know this may work for a small percentage of people, but if you're like most, it's a train wreck waiting to happen.

Not only do most New Year's resolutions not work, but you also take a serious hit to your self-confidence as well as your happiness. You start out all gung-ho, ready to change and shift your entire life. Maybe you are trying to lose weight, make more money, or just set out to be a happier person.

The problem lies in how we are all programmed and how we've evolved since the beginning of time. We are habitual people. Our habits are what can change our entire lives.

The problem is we have evolved very slowly. It's not like we popped out of a cave and invented cell phones. No, this took a very long time. We were once programmed purely for survival. As time progressed, we evolved from the Stone Age to the Bronze Age, then the Iron Age, Machine Age, Atomic Age, and Technology Age.

It took a very long time for us as people on this earth to go from cavemen to having a cell phone in our hand with almost limitless information.

So why do most people think they can completely change their life because the clock strikes midnight and it's now a New Year? I get it; it's exciting to think of all the new possibilities available to you within the next year.

And you can truly change your entire life in a year—and in many cases much less than that.

Your mind, just like your body, can be completely changed, but it's not a flip-the-switch sort of situation. Let's say you make a New Year's resolution to go to the gym every day. January 1, you are in that gym, busting your ass, sweating up a storm. Day 1 of working out felt great. You felt on top of the world.

Day 2 rolls around, and you realize you haven't worked out in years. You are sore and your muscles hurt in places you didn't know existed. You have thoughts racing through your head. "I'm sore. I don't feel good. Maybe I should take a day off and let my body rest."

You know what happens next ... soon enough, you're eating like crap again, you're not working out, and you fall right back into your old habits, and your New Year's Resolution goes to shit.

Sound familiar? I'm sure it does. It's not just you. You've been doing the same thing for so many years that a lot of your actions and behaviors have become automatic.

We're not programmed for rapid shifts for our own protection. You see, if we were able to shift that rapidly, our society would have never evolved. We would have all died.

If cavemen were like, "Fuck it, I'm out of this cave," without first learning how to survive outside of a cave, they surely would have died. Maybe from an animal, sickness, or who knows what? It was a scary world back then.

It took small shifts over long periods of time for us to get to where we are today. That's how evolution works. To think you can just somehow willpower through and change your entire being overnight is a bit far-fetched.

I spoke about the 1% shift earlier in this book, and that is exactly what I am talking about. If you can be one percent better today than you were yesterday, you start to create momentum, and you start moving forward.

The funny thing about momentum is that it compounds. If you can keep that wheel spinning forward, you can be in an entirely different place in a short period of time. Just don't try to do it all at once.

CHAPTER TWENTY-TWO

How to Save Millions by Spending Money

You read that title right. I am saying if you want to make money, you have to spend it. Not only that, but if you don't spend it, it may end up costing you millions of dollars.

Let's lay out a scenario for you with two people. I'll use myself as one character: Jared, the cheap-ass (true story), and Bob, the spender. Bob will be the one who decides to spend his money (on the right things, i.e., not hookers and blow).

Both Jared and Bob, are smart, resourceful, hard workers. They decide that they need to change their lives.

Both of them decide to go down the same path of starting a business, but this is where their paths differ.

Jared (the cheap-ass) decides that he doesn't need to hire a coach or mentor. He uses Google and YouTube to gather knowledge. The problem Jared has is information overload. Yes, all the information you could ever need can be found here, but you have to look at so many different pieces of information to try to piece together a plan. Slowly, Jared starts to figure it out after months/years of putting all the pieces of the puzzle together.

Bob is smart. He decides he wants to change his life. He finds someone who has done exactly what he wants to do and pays this person to give him the EXACT path he needs.

Jared and Bob both get to the same place. The difference is TIME. If we factor time into the equation, it looks like this:

Bob decides to start a business, hires a mentor, and, within 12 months (because he follows a laid-out plan), has made his first million.

Jared decides to start a business, goes to Google/YouTube, spends endless hours researching and taking notes, goes into information paralysis, finally figures out what to do, and within 12 months has just gotten his business off the ground but not made any real money.

So let's break down those numbers: Bob spent $10,000 and at the end of the year, he had $990,000. Jared spent $0, but at the end of the year, he had made $20,000.

So if you look at it from an outside perspective, Bob may have spent $10,000 to start, but it cost Jared $980,000. Yes, it cost Jared almost a million dollars in the negative over a year because he wanted to try to figure it out himself.

That is only the beginning because Bob now has a million dollars and a year's head-start over Jared. As the years pass, the gap between these two incomes is only going to get greater and greater.

Now, you may think this is some hypothetical, rags-to-riches story where the hero starts from nothing, hustles his ass off, and finally makes it, but this is actually my story.

Every failure has a lesson. I know this. So I am not one to regret things, but—and this is a huge but—I wish I had sought help sooner because I didn't make my huge strides as both a person and a businessman until I found some mentors.

I had been reading business books, searching for ideas online, and chasing every shiny object I could since I was 16, but I didn't make any real money till I was 31 years old. This was because I got paralyzed by information. I was a perpetual information gatherer but not a doer. I never had a clear path, so nothing much got accomplished. I just kept researching.

I found my first real mentors when I was around 29 years old. This is when I really started working on me. It took several years working on me and my mindset before I was prepared to dive into business. I found several other mentors through this first mentor and eventually found the one who would change my life. Every person was somehow linked, and it wasn't until I found this group that my life changed.

If there was one thing I would have done differently it would be finding help sooner and starting sooner. In the scenario above, if I had started at 18, I would have been light years ahead of where I am now.

That's why I created a community of people just like you with lessons and training to help guide you along your path. You can get more information by going to definingmyhappiness.com.

Let me say it one more time. *People* are the most important resource you have.

I guarantee that no matter what you want in life, there is a person who has done it, and if you find that person and learn from them, you will cut years off the time it takes to figure things out on your own.

I wish I could drive this home in a way that would help you fully get how important this is. To give you an idea as to why this is so important ... I have been reading business books and studying real estate since I was 16 years old.

I worked tirelessly over and over, trying to put the pieces to the puzzle together. It wasn't until I was almost 30 years old that I started to figure this shit out. 14 YEARS!

Guess how I finally got my ducks in a row? I paid a person who had done what I wanted to do, and he gave me a system that I could replicate and follow. Once that PERSON stepped into my life, I finally was able to make some decent progress. It had its ups and downs, but at least I had a path.

I'm telling you right now if you don't have a path, you will go into mental masturbation.

What does that mean?

You will endlessly look for information trying to put all those pieces of the puzzle together only to never get moving because you go into information overload.

That's why I said at the beginning, I would wish more for the right person to walk into my life than having money.

Once you receive and implement the knowledge from the person helping you, the money will follow with a lifetime of benefits.

That's why I'm writing this book. Maybe I am that person for you. Maybe this is exactly what you need, right here, right now, to help you in your life. This may give you those benefits of knowledge that will last you a lifetime.

CHAPTER TWENTY-THREE

How to Design Your Journey by Defining Your Happiness

Do you remember being five years old?

I'm sure you at least remember snippets of it, but the real question is:

Do you remember being unhappy at five years old?

I don't think many people can remember being unhappy at age five. Even if you had a less than perfect upbringing and things were difficult, you don't necessarily remember it being bad. It wasn't till you started to become more conscious as you got older that you understood whether things were good or bad or if you were happy or unhappy.

I have two kids, and although they've had their moments and temper tantrums, they could flip the switch and go right back to happily playing even after having an utter meltdown. Even my youngest son who spent a good bit of his childhood in and out of the hospital with multiple surgeries was always able to revert back to being happy very quickly.

That's what I am trying to do with these lessons. (No, I'm not trying to make you have a tantrum, you smart ass.)

I want you to be able to flip that switch like a five-year-old going from tantrum to happy. It may not be in an instant like a five-year-old, but you can learn to figure out what makes you tick and what makes you happy.

Only as we get older do we seem to label things bad or good. When you're a kid, almost anything can become a game. Even if they lose that game, the bad feeling only lasts for moments—not hours or weeks or years.

If you're like me, you have struggled to find that happy medium, not labeling things as good or bad but treating them as guideposts for your life. A lot of what I am trying to teach you is how to train your brain to become like a five-year-old brain again ... before outside sources were able to taint what you know is true.

Life will always have ups and downs. Think of it this way: if you never had the downs, would you even know what the ups of your life were? It would be like a monotone person giving a speech—you would have no idea whether you should clap, boo, cheer, or cry.

For so long, I thought I should be happy 24/7, and if I wasn't, there was something wrong with me. This led me to a downward spiral of depression where I would stay in a funk for months at a time.

Now, I'm not saying you should hope to be unhappy. What I am saying is that you can use it as a GPS of sorts. If you start feeling unhappy or depressed, you should start looking for some guideposts to show what's going on in your life that are triggering those emotions.

Once you see what the issue is, you can correct it and flip that switch like a five-year-old and get back to that happy place.

I think happiness is the true spirit of all of our lives. As we get older and life becomes a bit more complicated, we tend to stress and worry—things a five-year-old never does.

Money eliminates some of the simple stresses of life, but it doesn't eliminate all of them. It amplifies a lot of things, making them 100 times more stressful than when we were broke.

I can tell you this, though, as I learned the hard way: if you can't figure out how to be happy while you're broke, you will be miserable even when you're "rich."

After I sold my company and moved my family across the country, I thought I would find my happy place. Turns out, it didn't make as much of a difference as I was hoping. I still had the same battles in my head, I still struggled to wake up some days, and to be honest, I really wasn't all that much happier. Of course, it was exciting to move and see so many new things, but once that wore off? Then what?

Sure, some things were better, but I was still the same me on the inside. So I looked deep inside and tried to figure out what was going on. Why was I still not happy? What was I missing?

What I found was I had set out on a path many years before, a path that was not a journey but only had one endpoint. Once I made it to that endpoint, what was I to do? I had no idea.

What I did was exactly what I have outlined in this book. I went through all my lessons I just wrote for you—honestly, I wrote them for me to see where I needed to point myself and what direction to head.

I became the five-year-old I had lost touch with. I became *me* again. I let people into my world. I made meaningful relationships. I let go and had fun again.

By doing this, I gave myself the gift of feeling okay with being me, and feeling like a five-year-old who had an amazing family that loved him.

I found my happiness and purpose at the same time. I realized the reason I couldn't get out of bed—the reason I felt unhappy—was because I had no direction. I had done everything I set out to do, but it was a hollow victory that left me more confused than when I started.

I went on this epic journey and only now do I realize it was a journey. At the time, I only saw "I'll be happy when ...." The problem was that I wasn't ever happy when I got there.

Finding my happy place did not come from money or moving. It came from finding me. And helping other people. And letting them in. By finding a group of people who support me and whom I support as well.

I found direction in what I wanted to do and that also brought me immense joy.

I found my purpose by helping others—helping others train their minds, start businesses, or grow their current business. I figured out that I get an extreme amount of joy by helping other people succeed in whatever they are trying to accomplish. The look on someone's face when they break through that barrier or start making more money or are just happy is the most amazing feeling in the world not only for them but also for me.

So what is your internal GPS trying to tell you?

What do you need to change?

Where should you be headed with your life?

When do you decide to begin your own journey?

Happiness comes to those who decide they want it. Much like anything in life, you need to figure out what makes you happy. I wish I could give you a magic pill, but it doesn't work quite like that.

Take a look at your life right now. Are you happy?

I want you to measure backward. What are the good things happening in your life right now or previously?

When you look back, what gives you the most joy? Is it your family? Is it something you've accomplished? Really feel the good times that you have experienced, put yourself in that time and place, and close your eyes.

Now, open your eyes. How did it feel to experience those amazing times again? It felt good, right? What about those times made you smile?

Start doing more of that. Whatever it was that made you smile, do that right now!

Now we are going to deal with where you are currently to where you want to be. A lot of unhappiness stems from the gap between where you are and where you want to be. You think you should make more money, be healthier, have more freedom, etc.

Because of this gap, you get lost and don't know what to do first. You know you should be doing something else but can't muster the strength to do that other thing. Every day you get more and more frustrated because you think you should be at that destination already. Without ever starting, though, you never get any closer to this place, so you stay exactly where you are, which causes more and more internal animosity.

First, we need to figure out what you want. I want you to think about one thing you want to accomplish. What is that one thing that you are unhappy with that you have been meaning to do or start? This needs to be something specific. It can NOT be, "I want more money (better: I want to make $250,000 by an exact date)." It can NOT be, "I want a better body (better: I will lose 25 pounds by this exact date)." You need a measurable, quantifiable goal.

I know what you're thinking; isn't this going to lead to "I'll be happy when …?" But we are going to do this in a certain way to make it a journey, which will also make it a process that you can celebrate all along the way.

On a piece of paper draw a long horizontal line.

|---|

On the left side put where you are currently. All the way on the right, put your goal.

Now, all along this line, put marks in it like so.

|------|------|------|------|------|------|------|------|------|------|----|

On each one of these vertical lines, I want you to work backward from your goal by putting guideposts of what needs to be done to get where you want to go.

This does a couple of things: it breaks down a larger goal into small, quantifiable results. By doing that, you don't get overwhelmed. Think of this as a journey map. Your job is not to try to swing out of the park and hit a home run. You're just trying to swing singles to be one percent better than you were yesterday. That's it.

I suggest getting a new notebook or journal and drawing this out on page one. Every single day I want you to write down how you were one percent better than you were yesterday. I want you to celebrate each day that you were 1% better and 1% closer to your goal.

By doing this—by actually taking the time to draw out a plan and then keeping track—you are making your own guideposts. By having guideposts, your GPS never gets lost. By tracking how you were 1% better today versus yesterday, you are breaking down this one big thing into a journey of steps. Steps that you can celebrate.

Each day, you will see progress, and by seeing each day individually, you won't see this big goal and think, "I'll be happy when ..." You will see progress, and you will see you are moving closer and closer to where you want to be, which will give you purpose.

You will start to gather momentum, and once you start rolling down that hill, no one can stop you.

AFTERWORD

"I'll Be Happy When … "

Those are the words that cursed a good majority of my life.

I call it "The Happiness Curse." A curse that affects more people than we realize. A curse that makes you think there is some sort of end game. Like you can finish this game called life and finally win.

I think every single person who reads this book can win in life, but there is no point where you will say to yourself, "I'm finished." If you are finished, it means you've completed something, and the only way to complete life is to no longer live it.

Life is constant change, and through that change, you are living. What is up to you is whether you decide to enjoy this process and learn to love the journey.

If you can learn to not place an end goal on things, you will enjoy the process a lot more. It's not easy, but if you don't start slowing down to have some fun along the way, what is the point of this whole thing called life anyway?

I want you to do one thing tonight before you go to bed.

As you're lying there, think of 10 things that you appreciated about today. They could be as simple as a moment shared with your child or spouse.

It could be as simple as, "I appreciate that I woke up this morning."

Count on your fingers ten things you appreciated about today.

Do this every night before you go to bed and watch your world completely transform.

YOUR NEXT STEPS

So where does this leave you?

The reason I wrote this book was to help you. Unfortunately, though, you can only fit so much information into a book.

I've done some amazing things in my life and I have finally found my purpose, and that purpose is to help people just like you. I don't know where you are in life, but the easiest way to get from where you are now to where you want to be is to have someone help guide you in the process.

I'm not big on regrets, but if I did have one it would be that I wish I would have sought help sooner. I know it's not easy to break down that wall and ask for help. I've been there—you think you can conquer your mind, this world, and your life on your own.

What if I told you a little secret that took me years of frustration to learn on my own? You are not alone. Whatever it is you're dealing with right now, someone else has probably been there, they've done what you want to do, and they've gotten through the issue you are facing.

Not only has someone else dealt with what you're dealing with, but they have also gotten to the other side and learned the lessons so you don't have to struggle through figuring it out.

That's why I built an online community of people just like you, a community where you can find help and information on what you are trying to accomplish. The community is called "Defining My Happiness," and that's just what it was designed to do: help you define your happiness and help you find your happy place.

Like I said in the beginning, this book can only hold so much information. Yes, I could have written a 500-page book, but it would have been intimidating and you may not have even made it this far in the book.

That's why I created this community, not only so you could meet others just like you who are dealing with the same issues but also meet people who have found solutions to those issues. It also includes video lessons that break things into small steps to help guide you in the right direction. In the group, I do weekly live trainings where you can ask me questions and get direct answers from me on the issues you are facing.

We will break down how to Define Your Happiness and figure out what makes you tick so you can get to your own "Happy Place." For most people, finding that "Happy Place" includes regaining their freedom back to live a life worth living.

You will get access to my "How to Start Your Online Business and Take Your Freedom Back by Designing A Life Worth Living" course. This will walk you through how to take your first steps to start that business. I will show you how to work backward so you can design your dream life.

I want to change your "I'll be happy when" to "I'll be happy now." There is only one time to start, and that is *now*. So come join us on this journey by visiting www.definingmyhappiness.com and getting started.

I look forward to seeing you on the other side.

ABOUT THE AUTHOR

After building a life most people only dream of, Jared Springer realized he was no happier than when he started. This set him on a mission to figure out why he would always catch himself saying, "I'll be happy when ... "

Jared Springer began his journey as an entrepreneur at the age of nine, detailing cars at dealerships after school with his Dad until midnight. The work ethic he learned would serve him well on the road ahead. As an adult, he found himself working a full-time job while struggling to run his own businesses until the day his body gave up on him.

He woke up one morning unable to walk. After being rushed into the emergency room, he was given two choices: have emergency back surgery, or never walk again. It wasn't a hard choice. What followed would transform his life and his very being.

No longer able to work a job, he was forced into full-time self-employment just to feed his family. With $20, a YouTube education, and a dream of making a million dollars in one year, Jared Springer once more took steps on his entrepreneurial journey.

He began with books; *he knew books.* He went to Goodwill with $20, bought 20 books for $1 each, and listed them on Amazon. In turn, he sold them for over $50.

He repeated this process over and over again for months until he made enough to start his own brand and create his own products. Jared was hell-bent on achieving his goal of making one million dollars in one year … *and he did.*

After building businesses from scratch and selling them, Jared realized that he had some very unique skills. Combining those skills with clinical burnout from the business world drove him to start writing a tale of self-discovery to determine the direction to point his life.

As he began to tell his story on paper, he realized that his book could help other people who were making the same mistake of delaying life's enjoyment until reaching a certain point. His experience taught him that even when people reach their "I'll be happy when" point, they still wouldn't be happy unless they figure out what makes them tick.

He realized quite a few things while writing this book. One thing in particular is that he loves teaching and watching other people grow. He gains more enjoyment from seeing other people become successful than from his own achievements. He also realized his innate ability to see what others can't—especially when it comes to mindset, business, and marketing, and how all three are inextricably intertwined.

Since these discoveries, Jared has been coaching, teaching, and helping others from all over the world learn how to find happiness while expanding their business and increasing their income in the process.

Jared Springer has lived in every corner of the U.S. He was born in Wisconsin, grew up in California, moved to Florida, followed by Georgia, and eventually found his way back to his birthplace. Currently, he resides in St. George, Utah with his wife Sara and two children, Sebastian and Isaac.

ACKNOWLEDGMENTS

I want to thank the mentors who have had the biggest hand in changing my life. Without their guidance, I don't know if I ever would have been able to find my way.

Sean Whalen: Thank you from the bottom of my heart. You opened my eyes to a different way of thinking. I never knew how much honesty and accountability could change my life. I could still be stuck down the rabbit hole of self-pity if it weren't for you. My mess is my message, and, without you, I don't think I would have had the courage to write this book.

Ryan Daniel Moran: I don't think words could describe my appreciation for you. I was lost without a path. You laid out that path, and it took me to levels of success I could never imagine.

Jesse Elder: Your teachings helped shape my mind. Without learning how to control my own thinking, none of what I have done could have been remotely possible.

Ryan Stewman: I have learned so much from you throughout the years. It started first with your sales, real estate, and social media marketing training, and as the years passed, the amount of knowledge and skills I have learned from you have helped me in every area of my life.

Garrett J. White: Thank you for creating Wake Up Warrior. I have lived the Warrior's way for almost eight years now. Your framework for how to live your life transformed mine several times when I needed it most. The discovery of the Warrior's Way was the catalyst that propelled me first to make a change in my life, which set in motion a life of expansion and growth for me. Thank You.

Sebastian and Isaac: The lessons I've learned from being a father to both of you have been immeasurable. You gave me a purpose when I was lost. Your love and strength are amazing. I am honored to be your father! I love you and thank you both!

Larry Springer: Thank you, Dad, for instilling in me a work ethic that has served me well for years. You pushed me to be a better man at a young age, and I have carried that with me my entire life.

Kim Sutherland: Mom, you taught me to be a dreamer—always curious for what this world offered. I know you are still looking down and smiling and guiding me even though you are no longer with us.

I also want to give a special thanks to everyone who helped shape this book by taking the time to read it and offer helpful advice. Thank you to Anthony and RaeLyn Simmons, Todd Sandberg, Randall Brinkerhoff, Ian Adams, Nicholas Vescovi, and Sara Springer.

Lori Lynn: Thank you for taking my scrambled words and chicken scratch and helping turn it into a book. Without your guidance and help at every step of the way, I don't think we would have ever made it to print. You were more than an editor, you were a mentor and friend throughout the entire process encouraging me to keep going even when I was scared to let my story into the world. You encouraged me to keep going because you saw how many people my story could help.

Made in the USA
Coppell, TX
25 January 2021